JESUS CHRIST IN THE BUSINESS WORLD

IGNATIUS FERNANDEZ

JESUS CHRIST in the Business World

© All rights reserved. No part of this book may be reproduced or transmitted in any form or by any means, electronic or mechanical, including photocopying, recording, or by any information storage and retrieval system, without written permission from the author, except for the inclusion of brief quotations in a review.

JESUS CHRIST in the Business World
Ignatius Fernandez
Copyright 2018 by Ignatius Fernandez
ISBN: 978-0-9763815-3-2

Printed and bound in America
Easton-Books Small Press Publishing, Murphy, Texas
All media and inquiries please visit:
http://Easton-Books.com

This book is designed to provide information and motivation to readers. It is sold with the understanding that the publisher is not engaged in rendering any type of psychological, legal, or other professional advice. The content of each chapter is the sole expression and opinion of the author, and not necessarily that of the publisher. No warranties or guarantees are expressed or implied by the publisher's choice to include any of the content in this volume. Neither the publisher nor the individual author shall be liable for any physical, psychological, emotional, financial, or commercial damages, including, but not limited to, special, incidental, consequential or other damages. Our views and rights are the same: You are responsible for your own choices, actions, and results.

~First Edition~

ACKNOWLEDGEMENTS

As a senior manager for many years, I interacted with other senior managers, in the companies I worked for, and with executive management in competitor companies. I learned from them. I was fortunate to have some good bosses. They taught me some lasting lessons. Some bosses were difficult, more interested in themselves, and not in the company or in others. From them, I learned lessons on what not to think or do. My management education did not come just from business school.

In this book, I have tried to link what I profited from management experience, with what I gained from the teachings of Jesus. His 2000-year-old lessons resonate with some I had from Industry, some from my teaching experience in business school, and some from the training sessions I conducted for senior managers.

Dr. Wayne Norton, in his Foreword, has explained the merits of the book in words that are hard to match. It appears that he journeyed with the group of managers in the plot. I thank him for delving into the conversations among the managers, to surface with hard-hitting facts on management. His pointed reference to the wealth in the teachings of Jesus, and its relevance today, reinforces the points the book makes.

The reviewers have done a praiseworthy job in studying the book in a short time and deploying their skills to project the book in its true light – *"a must-read for students of management and practitioners"*, in the words of Edward Valenzuela, former Managing Director, Accenture. I thank the reviewers for their time and effort. Their surnames appear in alphabetical order, below extracts from their reviews, just after the front cover of the book, and on the back cover.

On my own, I could not have written such a book. I needed the wisdom and power of the Holy Spirit. He guided me through the different stages of the book to make it what it is: a treasure trove of the teachings of Jesus for the business world, mined from the Holy Bible, the Catholic Edition. I hope that readers will find nuggets of wisdom in it to apply to their work situations.

I thank my family for encouraging and supporting me in this attempt. And, I thank the publisher for her unconditional cooperation.

God bless you.
Ignatius Fernandez

JESUS CHRIST in the Business World

Extracts from reviews–surnames appear in alphabetical order.

*Since the book is nonfiction that reads like fiction it is even more exciting to read. What a great vision and concept Fernandez! **James Manning** – James the Watchman, Minister, Author, Tampa, Florida.

*A group of managers discovers Jesus Christ, as presented in the four Gospels, through the principles he taught to help the business world. Their journey with Jesus is not a haphazard course of religious expectations or demands. Quite the contrary, they find an opportunity to assimilate ideas from many schools of thought on management and leadership. **Dr. Wayne Norton,** Founder, and Executive Director - Hope for Your Day Ministries. Claremore, Oklahoma.

*Ignatius Fernandez has produced a scholarly and absorbing analysis of how Jesus Christ's behavior sets an example, not just for our personal lives, but also for our professional conduct, and gives a compelling and rigorous account of how Jesus was in fact the definitive leader in every respect. **Paul Sellers,** former Director, British Council, London.

*Mr Fernandez has succeeded in the obviously difficult task of situating the life and ministry of Jesus Christ, in an ambience where the events and incidents which occurred two thousand years ago, assume a remarkable contemporary meaning and relevance. Jesus, as an exemplary human being, rather than Jesus, the Son of God, is the term of reference throughout. **Professor S. Swaminathan,** former Business Editor, The Hindu Newspaper, Chennai, India.

*By incorporating the talents and skills of Jesus as a leader and manager of men, in a story of a company that is trying to change its corporate culture, the author weaves into an interesting plot, the essence of management and leadership principles. **Edward Valenzuela,** Former Managing Director, Accenture LLC. Littleton, Colorado.

*Apart from the immense efforts that have gone into the writing of the book by Mr Ignatius Fernandez, what comes through the pages of the book is his genuine admiration, love and warmth for the human nature of Jesus Christ. **Louis Xavier s j.,** Former Director, Loyola Institute of Business Administration (LIBA), Chennai, India.

CONTENTS

Foreword	1
01) Appraisal Time – 10.35	3
02) The Role Model	11
03) The Gospels	20
04) 2000 years ago	27
05) Jesus - Fully Human and Fully Professional	36
06) Relationship with the Team	54
07) The people person	64
08) Perceptions of the model	70
09) Some lessons for professionals	74
10) Jesus appraised	84
11) Sink or sail together	96
12) The Need to Change	101
13) The Change Agent	112
14) Jesus – the unrivalled Communicator	120
15) Leadership and Change	127
16) A formidable combination	132
17) Doing the right thing	139
18) Having new eyes	150
References	i
Author Page	iii

THE FOREWORD

One of the greatest blessings of an almost fifty-year ministry has been my friendship and fellowship with Ignatius Fernandez. He is a man of scholarly achievement, and integrity, and a theologian of great insight. As a professor of leadership and management, he brings a new insight into the business world. As a theologian and dynamic man of God, he has a deep insight into the New Testament, which is so evident in his recent book on Christology – THINK CHRIST, LIVE CHRISTIAN.

The excitement in JESUS CHRIST IN THE BUSINESS WORLD swells, as a fictional business leader and his group of managers are invited on a journey to meet Jesus Christ in the Business World. This business leader and his group of managers - people with different backgrounds, different religions, and different schools of leadership - decide to study the four New Testament Gospels. With that decision, a brilliant and captivating conversation emerges. The managers discover Jesus Christ, as presented in the four Gospels, through the principles he taught to help the business world. Their journey with Jesus is not a haphazard course of religious expectations or demands. Quite the contrary, they find an opportunity to assimilate ideas from many schools of thought on management and leadership. The author provides a podium from which Jesus speaks, a landscape on which Jesus ministers, and a forum from which Jesus listens. Each chapter opens with a very relevant and valuable quotation to engage us in the subject that follows. The wisdom of Jesus Christ is shared in the form of the *"Golden Rule":* a company that satisfies its employees will satisfy its customers; all-round satisfaction is attempted. One of the characters in the plot, through whom the author speaks, declares: *"The way I see it, Jesus is not ancient. Jesus is ageless."* This statement leads to extensive research on the relevance of Jesus' teachings to the Business World. Empathy and compassion were hallmarks of Jesus' leadership, as He interacted with people. It is not surprising that they become the platform for leadership.

Fernandez reminds us that leaders must dare to be true to who they are, where they are, and with whom they are. Integrity, seen in the life of Jesus, is a *"must"* for leaders. Today's business professional has many challenges like staying positive in perception, in projection, and in people-skills. In tune with such challenges, the author presents *"The 360-degree appraisal"* as a unique and amazing tool - a system that conducts employee evaluation in a *"win-win"* fashion. The author also reflects on *"Situational Management,"* which is another effective method that Jesus used. In a walk with Jesus Christ in the Business

World, a great adventure awaits us - of learning, of growing, and of opening our hearts and minds to new possibilities. Jesus Christ taught on sound relationships. The powerful words of people, valuable experiences with people, and profound impact upon people are available to us when the teachings of Jesus Christ are allowed into the area of business. Fernandez greatly helps us to become better managers and leaders as he escorts us on this journey of relationships – charted by Jesus. Fernandez quotes Marcel Proust as he opens the last chapter, *"The real voyage of discovery consists not in seeking new landscapes, but in having new eyes."* Thank you, Fernandez, for helping us have *"new eyes"* in the business world, and in our lives!

Dr. Wayne Norton, Founder/Executive Director Hope for Your Day Ministries, Claremore, Oklahoma, USA

Chapter One: Appraisal Time – 10:35

"Nothing is as easy as it looks. Everything takes longer than you think. If anything can go wrong, it will." Murphy's Law

Mount Pharmaceuticals, Chennai, India, has a short history of nineteen years, in two parts. The first part, of fourteen years, was not smooth sailing. Like a ship caught in a storm, it was buffeted by strong winds and rocked violently. The crew feared for their lives. Miraculously, the ship came out of the storm and was not wrecked. Even today, they are not able to explain the escape from disaster. The second part of five years under a new CEO, brought about stability and marked growth. Two years ago, the Initial Public Offering (IPO), was over-subscribed. With some money in the company, the new CEO and his team of senior managers pumped in hope, buoyancy, and gave the company a definite direction. Healthier results soon followed, and the company experienced growth. Despite its troubled past, the biggest strength of the company was its team of managers – committed, full of zeal and forward-looking professionals.

The product-range was nothing special, with the exception of two recent product launches for the treatment of heart conditions. These new offerings achieved an immediate, positive response. The product range also included diuretics, drugs for hypertension, drugs for the treatment of diabetes, a few antibiotics, and some dietary supplements. In all, there were thirty-two products. Market penetration improved as the distribution network expanded. Research and Development were tardy, but plans were underway to pick up the pace. The recent export-activity showed positive signs.

Customer-feedback was not overwhelming but was generally good. The new CEO and management team were determined to roll out new products and chart a growth trajectory. They needed a stimulus; it would come to them in an out-of-the-ordinary way.

Lambert Kurien, Vice President of Marketing, was busy during the weekend, not with personal chores, but with professional duties with a bearing on his career. He worked on his Annual Appraisal Form and gave it finishing touches. He repeatedly went over facts and figures from notes he carried in his briefcase and data on his laptop. The year had been good. Targets were met. Market share had increased, and he had every reason to be happy with the performance of his team. After hours of work on the Form, he was satisfied and shut it.

On Monday morning, he stepped out of his spacious four-bedroom, second-story apartment, ready for an eventful day at the office. Lissy, his wife, was dressed in a dark green saree, adorned with a gold border and a matching blouse. Her black, bouncy, shoulder-length hair, falling carelessly along her cheeks, gave her a saucy look. She looked attractive. She wished him well and waved goodbye, smiling warmly as she shut the door. She then walked into their prayer-space, the enthroned picture of Jesus, and offered a short prayer for her husband.

Lambert walked towards the elevator, changed his mind and took the steps to the ground floor. Ravi, his chauffeur over the last three years, let the recently acquired black VW Jetta glide into the driveway. He scrambled out from behind the wheel and opened the rear door. Lambert's six-foot-one frame slid effortlessly into the rear leather seat, with his briefcase snugly at his side. Depending on traffic, the drive to the office would take about twenty minutes.

Monday mornings were usually busy with meetings, but today Lambert Kurien was relatively stress-free. He sat back, unbuttoned his Armani Jacket, and smiled as he adjusted his sunglasses. He was looking forward to a good day. He knew that his appraisal would fetch him positive remarks. At 10:35 he was scheduled to meet his boss, the CEO, Joseph D'cruz. Joseph fixed odd times for discussions. It was never 10:30 or 11:00. It was 10:35 or 11:03. Why? Lambert never knew, but 10.35, was okay. In fact, he had set the entire morning aside for Joseph.

Ravi sensed the mood of his boss and quietly slipped in Vivaldi's Four Seasons. As notes from the speakers filled the car, Lambert smiled again. Vivaldi's music for springtime was just right. He knew as he got to the office, there would be more than a spring in his step. As Lambert looked outside, he noticed malls were being decorated with festoons, buntings and Santa Claus. It was about three weeks to Christmas. He remembered, his eight-year-old son Augustus, had planned to write to Santa Claus for a bicycle. *'Bright colors, curved handlebar and all that'*, in Augustus' words. Lambert knew he must play Santa Claus by Christmas Eve.

At forty, Lambert was still young and energetic, and looked it. He thrived on challenges, tight-corner situations, and relished the success that followed. Not one to be laid-back and complacent, he accepted new tasks readily and involved himself fully. Perhaps Joseph made note of the new initiatives he had undertaken lately.

He joined the company as a young management trainee, right after finishing his post-graduation in Business Management; and opted for Marketing, doing the rounds with field staff for months, until he got his posting in Product Management. Then, it was a steady climb: Assistant Product Manager, Product Manager, Regional Manager, Marketing Manager. Now, he was Vice-President Marketing. The company has been good to him; he had no reason to complain.

The VW Jetta came to a halt in the office parking area. As Lambert stepped out of the car, he noticed Joseph's white BMW was not in its usual parking space. Joseph always drove his car to and from the office, with the chauffeur perched on the edge of the rear seat. At the office, the chauffeur took over the driving. Why would a CEO let his chauffeur sit watching, when he drove? Only heaven knew. Joseph was different in many ways and it took time to understand him.

Lambert walked to the elevator. Olivia Pinto, who was waiting in front of it, greeted him. She was in a purple salwar–kameez, a typical Indian outfit. Her hair was twisted in a bun at the top of her head. With a string of pearls and ear studs to match, and her sonata-like smile, that was more than winning, she looked gorgeous. The perfume she wore added to the effect.
"Will Mr. D'cruz be in shortly?"
"He has a meeting with Marcus Gomes, a member of our board. He should be back after the meeting."
"Thank you, Olivia."
They got into the elevator and ascended to the fourth floor in silence.

Lambert settled into his office. He called Ramona, his secretary, and quickly cleared papers she had left on his desk, on Friday. As he sipped his hot tea, he made a few phone calls and quickly answered some emails on his laptop. It was now 10:25; in ten minutes, his appraisal would start. Lambert was confident and had little to worry about his appraisal. To boost his confidence, he had, at times, taken on competition and bruised it. Yet this morning, there was a suggestion of anxiety. This would be his first appraisal since his promotion, and he knew Joseph could keep him guessing. At 10:33 he left his office, telling Ramona he would be with the boss. Then he strode into the passage leading to Joseph's office.

When Lambert Kurien was promoted last year, Ramona Jacob was moved from the regional office to the corporate office. She learned fast and seldom kept work pending. Lambert just loved that; for him, things had to be done now, right now. Ramona adjusted the belt around her slim waist and pulled down her bright yellow dress. She pushed back black hair in clumps from her face and squeezed her lips together to put on a fresh coat of lipstick. Then, and only then, Ramona got busy with her work.

Lambert smiled as he passed Olivia and moved into Joseph's office. It was 10:35.

"Ah, here you are, Lambert," said Joseph as his VP Marketing walked into his office.

"Yes, good morning," Lambert replied.

"Yes, please, sit down," Joseph waved and continued, "The last time we talked of your appraisal we were flying over Delhi."

"Yes, the time has come for us to talk." Lambert sounded more like a Hyde Park Preacher, as he handed Joseph his appraisal form.

Joseph pushed back his chair, crossed his legs, knotted his fingers, and looked Lambert in the eye. "Lambert, let's set the appraisal form aside and just chat for a while."

Lambert nodded.

"Tell me, how has this year gone?"

"The year is not over, but we have figures up to November."

"Tell me more about those figures."

"Sales have grown by over 9%. The two new products we launched have done exceptionally well, market share is still climbing. Traders are counting gains and the team is happy. The scorecard looks respectable."

"That's good to hear. As always, you enjoy the feel of success. Tell me more about your team."

"What would you want to know?"

"For starters, how have they accepted you?"

"You'll have to check with them."

"No, Lambert, I want your thoughts on it."

"Going by the way they respond to me, I don't think they have any apparent grouse."

"Why would you say that?"

"Well, I can't read their minds."

"True. Yes, that is true."

"Raphael, Sunil, and Laxmi seem to be okay with me."

"As your Marketing Managers, do they see you as a strong and dependable leader or (he was looking for words), do they regard you as a boss who was once a peer, their friend?"

"I imagine I am both to them."

"Can you explain that?" the CEO inquired.

"A few years ago, I read a book titled *"Leadership and The One-Minute Manager."* The authors write on situational management. They suggest, don't adopt a fixed style. Instead, adapt to the situation. I found the idea eminently suitable. With Raphael, I delegate. With Sunil, I have to be supporting. With Laxmi, I have to direct her, more because she was recently promoted."

"I recall reading that book. Good stuff." Joseph paused. And added, "But do you have trouble with adapting your leadership style?"

"In the beginning, yes, it was tough. It still is, but I am learning," Lambert confided.

"Are you satisfied?" Joseph persisted.

"I could be doing better," Lambert sounded cautious.

For the next twenty minutes, they discussed the rest of his team and his peers. Joseph seemed to be pleased with their discussion.

"And how is it with the market?" Joseph questioned.

"Right now, things are reasonably good. I meet the top doctors, with the regional managers, every quarter. I visit the traders and get feedback regularly. I visit large hospitals and negotiate with their purchase departments. I also ensure anything outside of the ordinary is brought to my attention immediately."

"Are you saying you have set up a system?"

"It's more of an informal thing."

"And how faithful is the system, how can you be sure it works?"

"I can never be absolutely sure, but by and large, it works."

Olivia moved in ghost-like, her exotic perfume coming in before she did, and left a tray with a gleaming teapot and cups. Then she disappeared, leaving a trail of her bewitching perfume. Joseph rose and poured the hot tea into the two cups. He offered one to Lambert and leaned back with his cup, perched on the edge of the table. Joseph reassured Lambert he had asked for tea and not coffee, knowing his preference. The teacups found their place back on the tray, and they got back to business.

"Lambert, I am beginning to believe that our relationships, more than anything else, determine our success."

"And how do I score?" Lambert probed.

"I'll come to that later," Joseph deflected, "Life is a network of relationships and that is not a cliché."

"I am inclined to agree," Lambert endorsed the boss.

"Our relationships are only as good as our communication. This idea was proposed by John Powell, the celebrated author, and I fully agree with him." Joseph commented.

Lambert got the feeling that his appraisal was being sidetracked. Joseph was on a roll and nobody stopped him when he decided to bounce ideas off you.

"You know, I have been doing some reading and some thinking. The time has come for me to share some thoughts with you."

Lambert quickly looked at his watch. It was 11:40, an hour and twenty minutes to lunch. He had set the morning aside for Joseph. So, he would have to stay and listen.

"Have you heard of the 360-degree Appraisal?" Joseph asked.

"Yes, but I haven't given it much thought."

"Richard, from HR, is sold on it. I like the looks of it. When we were in Business School it was only a topic. Now we have come face to face with it. I want to take a serious look at it."

Opening his top drawer, he pulled out the photocopy of an article. Very slowly and deliberately he gave it to Lambert. He had seen a similar article in a financial daily but somehow, he did not get to read it.

As Lambert read the article, Joseph called Olivia. He wanted her to follow up on a few points, then he dictated a mail. Lambert went through the illustration.

He thought it was a smart way of looking at relationships. It was rather different from the old way of just getting feedback only from the superior. Check with different sources: The boss, peers, subordinates, and customers. A multi-source appraisal looked fair to him.

Lambert looked up. "Yes?" he quizzed.

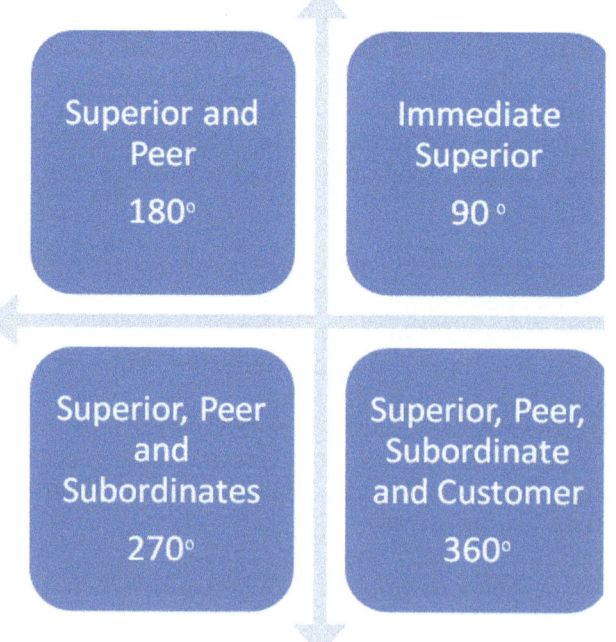

"What do you think of it?" Joseph asked.

"It seems interesting, but I don't recall how it works. Business School was a long time ago, and I did not specialize in Human Resources

"We need to get Richard to work on this initiative. In the west, the System is popular, with many companies adopting it. The system is simple, instead of depending only on the evaluation by the boss, feedback is also collected from peers, juniors, and customers. The 360-degree appraisal is the sum total of all feedback. Graphically it appears in four segments. The boss continues to be the final judge, but only after weighing inputs from others."

"We should examine it. Check it out." Lambert sounded reassuring.

"You know what we'll do? We'll put your appraisal on hold. Not for long, a few weeks perhaps." Lambert was not amused but nodded.

"We'll set aside time and Olivia will get back to you. We have to have a serious discussion."

"What is it about?" Lambert asked with little interest.

"This will affect our entire operations as professionals. We have to look at our roles to redefine them and choose an appropriate model."

"You are into riddles. What exactly do you mean?"

"You and I, Richard and the other VP's must meet, and I will share my thoughts with you."

"Very well, just tell me when." Lambert rose to leave.

Joseph joined him at the door. "Lambert set your worries aside on the appraisal. I know you have done well. I am putting off the exercise on purpose."

"If it's okay with you, it's okay with me." They shook hands and parted.

Joseph returned to his desk and called Olivia. She quietly entered his office. "Olivia, will you line up a meeting with all the VPs'? It's important and please, give them copies of this article." (The one he had shown Lambert).

"Is Wednesday afternoon at 3:55 okay with you?"

"You know my schedule. But how are they placed?"

"I have checked with the others. I still have to check with our VP Marketing."

"Warn them that the session could be a long."

"Yes, sir, I'll take care of it." Olivia went back to her desk.

In the VW Jetta on his way home, Lambert was pensive. Ravi, who had the music discs numbered, sensed the mood of his boss and promptly slipped in the second movement of Beethoven's Symphony No.6; right for the pensive mood.

Lambert tried to put his thoughts together: Joseph sounded rather mystifying, unlike him; he talked in riddles, yet he sounded reassuring. Funny how Murphy's Law still worked.

"Liz," Lambert turned to his wife as he sat sipping hot tea. "My appraisal has been put on hold."

"Why?" she was anxious.

"No problems, Joseph said he will do it in a few weeks."

"Did he tell you why?"

"Yes. He wanted to discuss something very important with all of the VP's."

"But surely it can't be your performance."

"Unlikely, we've had a good year."

"Has he been reading some new book? Is he trying to bring in some new idea?"

"Yes; but it is still early days." And added, "He said my appraisal was okay."

"Then stop worrying, everything will work out fine. Your hard work won't go unnoticed."

"Thank God, and thank you, Liz." Lambert grinned.

"If winter comes, can spring be far behind?" P. B. Shelley.

Chapter Two: The Role Model

"What single ability do we all have? The ability to change." L. Andrews.

Joseph D'cruz was a busy man. Crammed into each day was a tight schedule. With briefings, debriefings, a stream of emails and the rather continuous buzz on his smartphone, his diary was almost always packed. Tuesday was another busy day. Long meetings with Bill Foster, a contact from Singapore, and with the Secretary of Industries, State Government, kept him fully occupied the whole day. On Wednesday, Anjali, VP Finance and the Auditors met him in the morning. In the afternoon Joseph was rather tense. He was preparing for his session with the VPs, scheduled for 3:55. He had done his homework. At the meeting, he would kick start a thought-process, in fact, two. He would have to watch for initial reactions before going into details. How would it go? He was uncertain, yet he decided to go ahead.

Olivia walked in with a bunch of papers. He decided to check them right away. She waited, and as she waited, her eyes fixed on her boss. He was greying at the temples. The top of his head had certainly seen better days and he was beginning to put on some weight. His five-foot-six frame was not obvious due to his taste in clothes, which gave stature to his appearance. The man had been through tough times. Five years ago, when he took over as CEO, he was a young 39. Nobody down the line believed he could turn things around. Sales figures were pathetic, and morale was low. Banks refused to even meet with people from the company. Joseph came in like a breath of fresh air. Without complaining about the foul odor his predecessor had left, he set about expelling the stale air. He brought with him loads of enthusiasm, energy, and courage. He was clear-headed, systematic, accessible, friendly, polite, and honest. And, he never gave up. He often quoted Churchill – *"Never, never, never, never give up."*
Today, the company was endearingly called a blue-chip. There was a sense of well-being. Yet he believed his task was far from over, at forty-four, he had many dreams. The afternoon session would be the first of many to make those dreams come true.

"Olivia, nothing earth-shaking, except for an email to Bruno. Will you please take this down and send it to him right away?" He gave her a stack of papers and dictated a crisp reply. She was about to leave when he stopped her.
"Olivia, cheese sandwiches and coffee at 4:25, please. I know you will remember VP Marketing likes tea, not coffee."

"Yes sir, will there be anything else?"
"Yes, we don't want to be disturbed. Please take care of it for us."
"Yes, sir, I'll make sure you're not disturbed."

Joseph looked around his room. He felt good being the CEO. Although there were some regrets over avoidable mistakes, he felt good about the way things had gone since he took over the top slot. He wished he could have looked at things from the start in the way he did in recent times. Some changes could have been made earlier and the company could have more achievements. There was a tinge of sadness. Then he cast aside those thoughts and felt the buzz of the present; he was hopeful, even enthusiastic about the future. His eyes drifted to the message over the door: *"Never, never, never, never give up."* W. *Churchill.* He had not.

At 3:54 Olivia drifted in to say the VPs' were waiting in her room. Could they come in? "Yes, of course!" he boomed. George was the first to enter. The others quickly followed, as Joseph shook each one by the hand and in a low tone whispered: "Thank you. This is important."

They quickly found their seats in the corner of the CEO's office. Mini conferences were usually held here. Joseph took his seat. Facing him were George, Sammy, Anjali, Richard, and Lambert, the top five professionals directly reporting to him.

At 39, George Ferns was relatively young. His rise was meteoric. He picked up degrees and diplomas in India before doing a stint in the USA. He amazed his employers with his vast knowledge and skill at untangling twisted problems. He returned to India for personal reasons. After locating good schools for their children, he and his wife Veronica decided to settle in Chennai. He joined the team as a General Manager (Systems) and last year, he was promoted to Vice-President. With an agile mind, he worked on options fast; even in a crisis he was proactive and always a step ahead. What endeared him to others was his willingness to help those in need of his skills.

Sammy Ghosh, now 46, started at the bottom, on the shop floor. Diligently he learned fast and worked his way up the ladder. Along the way, he acquired a master's degree in Political Science, refusing to be left out of having a formal education. Sammy an avid reader, participated in every local seminar on manufacturing and materials to advance his knowledge. In the eyes of his peers he was a seasoned professional. He knew his area of work and gained the respect of his coworkers; even of competitors. To his wife Suman, he was unbeatable.

Anjali Kelkar was a Chartered Accountant with over twelve years of experience in Finance. She knew her subject. The auditors genuinely respected her knowledge and the bankers paid heed to her suggestions. It was rumored that she could check financial statements and spot flaws with ease. With her background, she could find a place on any top team. At 36, Anjali looked very secure. With her doting husband Suresh, she had every reason to be on top of the world.

Suave and sophisticated was Richard Rozario. At 42, he had some laudable achievements. He spent a few years in England where he acquired a fine taste in ties; nothing fancy, just stripes and spots. He was always well-groomed and courteous. In England, working in the area of Human Resources, he got a world view of this developing discipline. He was open to new ideas and had some fresh ideas of his own. One of his better ideas was to marry his boyhood sweetheart, Marion.

Joseph and Lambert attended the same business school, though some years apart.

Joseph surveyed the group again and smiled disarmingly. "Gentlemen and Anjali," he began, "today we could see the birth of some great ideas in our company. Our company needs your total cooperation. First, try to understand each idea. Second, give me your studied feedback. How we respond to the idea will determine our path. Once the idea is in the open, please feel free to speak your mind." He found them shifting in their seats, uncomfortable with the uncertainty, although they knew, with Joseph, they could be frank, even blunt; their relationships would not suffer.

"On Monday morning, the day before yesterday, Lambert and I discussed his appraisal. We did not finish the exercise. We shall be at it soon enough. During the discussion, we touched on an idea doing the rounds in many companies in India, the 360-degree Appraisal. You have with you some reading material Olivia sent you. Each employee, starting with me, will be appraised against feedback from his superior, his peers, his juniors and his customers. Put differently, appraisal only by the boss is no more enough. We need to know how we are seen by others. We need to assess our relationships, because the stronger the relationship, the better the transaction. And we are constantly transacting, with seniors, juniors, peers and external agencies. Functional transactions do not end by getting the job done. Like little bricks, they build the edifice of relationships with customers, vendors, colleagues, and superiors. By now, you know the System is popular in the West." Joseph stopped. There was silence. No one wanted to be the first to break it.

He did. "So far, we have not had professional feedback from anyone but the boss. The system was useful for a time. The time has come for a new idea. When the 360-degree appraisal is done well we can grow in key areas and build high-performing teams. When the appraisal is done poorly, it leads to mistrust, conflict and low morale. It's like the use of English, a vivid language. When used appropriately it's like a sweet-smelling bouquet of flowers. When used erroneously it stinks like decayed flowers. Perhaps Richard, who is articulate, could set the discussion in motion."

Smiling at Joseph in acknowledgment, Richard warmed to the idea. "I have some data, not enough, but I'm trying to get more information from companies in India with experience of using the 360-degree appraisal. Preliminary findings are encouraging, however only one in five have tried to implement it.

Those who have tried, find some merit in it. In England, I had the opportunity to introduce the system into a company. In India, the situation will not be the same. Traditional and cultural factors are different, making drastic changes difficult. By and large, we don't take kindly to negative feedback. We resent suggestions on how to improve and we are slow to change. If the system is to be introduced, we will have many hurdles to cross."

George was the next to respond. "It has a new angle to it, which appeals to reason. I am familiar with some of the American companies using the system."

Sammy: "Will this go down to the shop floor?"

Joseph: "We have to figure out if it will."

"The factory worker does not interact with customers and agencies," Sammy continued.

Anjali: "What's the catch? What are the hassles?"

"Count on the finance person to look for loopholes," Lambert joked.

Anjali: " Should we not approach this with caution?"

Joseph: "Of course, with abundant caution!"

Lambert: "To me, the idea looks good, especially for the marketing people. We only talk about customer satisfaction. We really don't get specific feedback from customers; this could be one way of doing it."

Joseph: "You have an excellent point. We have been shoddy in getting organized feedback from customers."

Anjali: "Are you saying raises and promotions will be based on such feedback?"

Richard: "As I said earlier, in India, we will have to adapt the System. The CSI and ESI are likely to be reckoning points".

Sammy: "What are CSI & ESI?" his voice curled with curiosity.

"Good question," answered Richard. "CSI stands for Customer Satisfaction Index and ESI is for Employee Satisfaction Index. The whole idea is to treat everyone we interact with as a customer: Customers, suppliers, agencies, peers, juniors, and so on. We broadly divide all such customers into two categories: The external customer and the internal customer. Unless the internal customer is satisfied, he may not satisfy the external customer. So, all-round satisfaction is important. Building relationships with all segments is important. Assessing how those relationships impact everyone's performance is important. Let me read a couple of quotations, one from the book *'Stop Paddling and Start Rocking the Boat'*, by Lou Pritchett.

'I firmly believe you cannot become a 100% customer-focused company until you've become a 100% employee-focused company. But the converse is also true. If you become a 100% employee-focused company, you almost certainly will become a 100% customer-focused company.'

'I have never seen a company that was able to satisfy its customers that did not also satisfy its employees. Your employees will treat your customers no better than you treat your employees.' Those were the words of Larry Bossidy, CEO of Honeywell. It means that an improvement in people management will reflect on the bottom line. Thompson, of Templeton College, Oxford, and Richardson, of the London School of Economics, presented a review of the most authoritative literature on the subject of People Management. The thirty-odd studies showed that good people management practices worked wonders for the bottom line."

Anjali: "I like the part on improving bottom lines. However, we need to tread carefully; this idea is rather complex."

Joseph: "You can say that again. The purpose of this meeting is to acquaint you with the idea. If you agree the idea is worth investigating, Richard will look into the details and get back to us."

Lambert: "With me it's go-go."

George: "Nothing wrong in checking it out."

Sammy: "Check. But let us be discreet. We don't want the shop floor thinking we are devising a tool to get rid of some of them."

Joseph: "You can be sure Richard will handle this discreetly."

Richard: "Thank you, Joseph, I'll do what I can."

Anjali: "Are we fixing any time-frame for the investigation?"

Joseph: "I think we'll leave it up to Richard."

Richard: "I'll need at least four to six weeks for some preliminary information."

Joseph: "Fine, we will look at this again in the third week of January."

Olivia came in, as scheduled, at 4:25. The sandwiches disappeared quickly, as did the coffee and tea. Was the meeting over? Did Joseph have anything else to say? The VP's looked at one another. In an attempt to gain time, Joseph cleared his throat, and ventured: "What do you think of Jesus? Jesus Christ?"

The startled look on their faces answered him.

Sammy, very strong in his Hindu beliefs, questioned, "What has Jesus got to do with us?" A shocked Anjali, another Hindu, was more guarded when she said: "We have heard of him."

George, "I am not sure how this question is relevant to our discussion on the 360-degree Appraisal."

Joseph responded fittingly. "Thank you, George, you have given me the right lead. We spoke of the 360-degree Appraisal and relationships. Just as water flows downhill into the river below, good relationships flow into the river of performance. Jesus is a model for relationship-building. We are professionals, can we learn something from him to improve our performance?"

Lambert, "Let us leave Jesus out of this; he is a Religious Head."

Joseph, "Are you suggesting religion and business are water-tight compartments?"

Lambert was apologetic, "Not really, but they are better when kept separate."

Joseph: "Shouldn't our beliefs guide us in our business? In our profession? Shouldn't they shape the way we act, react, and interact?"

Lambert, "Yes, of course, it goes without saying."

Joseph, "Why then this fear? I am not suggesting we look at Jesus as a Religious Head. We won't get into the spiritual side of Jesus or his Divine Powers. We plan to look at him as a man, as a professional, and a leader of his times. Is there something we can learn from him? If we can learn from Jack Welch and Bill Gates, why can't we learn from Jesus?"

Anjali, "Jack Welch and Bill Gates were managers of our time. We see them in the current context. Jesus lived 2000 years ago. He seems ancient."

Joseph, "You are right. He is an old-time leader and a professional. Can he give all-time leaders and professionals nuggets of wisdom? Could an American President of the 21st century look back at Abraham Lincoln and learn a thing or two? Or would he say Lincoln is ancient? The way I see it, Jesus is not ancient. Jesus is ageless."

Richard, "Very clever, Joseph, well said."

Joseph, "Thank you, Richard, all I ask of us is to keep an open mind. Can we shed our inhibitions and fears and look at Jesus, just as we would look at say, Steve Jobs, Ratan Tata or the Ambani brothers? How did he manage things 2000 years ago? Are there lessons for us? We shall not, I repeat, even remotely get involved in his Divinity."

Richard, "That sounds fair to me."

Joseph, "Let me share something with you only Teresa, my wife, knows. About six months ago I was in Delhi. I had to stay there for four days. I had nothing to read. Looking around the hotel room I spotted a copy of the Holy Bible. With nothing else to do, I began reading the New Testament - The Gospel of St. Mathew. By the time I got to chapter 5, I was hooked. I read all 28 chapters of Mathew.

I finished a late meal and then went out for a stroll. I found the Gospel of Mathew to be a fascinating study of a magnetic personality. The next evening, out of curiosity, I read the Gospel of St. Mark. During the next two evenings, I read Luke and John. I was enthralled, absolutely captivated. In the Gospels, the four writers record the life, words, and works of Jesus Christ, and I had read all the four. What I understood from the Gospels was that Jesus was a professional. He needed to come out of those pages and address us. What struck me was the incredible responsiveness of Jesus to his environment: the people, the happenings, the traditions, the practices. He was so alive to what was happening around him that he was never caught off guard."

"I have always believed that a good manager is first a good person, then and only then can he hope to be a good leader. As managers we transact, execute and stabilize. Now we need to graduate to becoming leaders, great leaders. The finish line is in sight, but there is a fair distance to travel. In Jesus, I found the sequence culminating. He shaped thought and action, ushering in a change leading to a transformation."

"I came back from Delhi and bought myself a copy of the Holy Bible. I read the 4 Gospels again and again. I have read them four times. I am looking forward to my fifth attempt. As a Christian I had not read the Gospels before. In humility, I admit to my lapse. My wife explained some passages that were not clear to me. Later, I met a few people who helped me clarify some of my doubts. Fr. Eric D' Mello, the Principal of my son's school was very helpful. He listened to me, spent time with me, and gave me some relevant reading material. I found the material enlightening. At the end of the study, I placed before myself a proposition, which I place before you: **Can Jesus give us a new way; a new template for running our business?** In business, we need advice, like we need when investing in the stock market. Can Jesus give us the right advice? Often, we are caught up in doing the necessary, the immediate and the urgent, but we miss out on doing the important. The time has come for us to seize the important. It's time to switch to enlightened corporate governance."

An uncomfortable silence descended on the group as each looked at others to spot signals to dispel their fear: were they going religious?

Olivia broke the silence as she looked in on the group. "Is there anything you need, sir? May I get you some more coffee, perhaps?" Joseph looked around. No one spoke. "No thank you, Olivia." As she stood there, Joseph's eyes signaled her on some action.

At last, Richard broke the silence, "I was not in the least prepared for such a turn in the discussions, but I see your point. We lose nothing by looking at a great man and checking if we can learn something from him."

Lambert, "Let's keep religion out."

Anjali: "I'm not too sure. I shall have to think about this situation. As of now, it sounds odd."

Sammy: "Same here."

George "I think Richard took the words out of my mouth: Why not study it?"

Joseph: "If there is some readiness to examine the idea, I'll give you some reading material."

Richard: "That is a good beginning." He rose to collect the papers Joseph held out; each set had a collection of seven articles.

- The Gospels
- 2000 years ago
- Jesus - Fully Human and fully Professional,
- Relationship with the Team.
- The people person
- Perceptions of the model
- Some lessons for Professionals.

Joseph: "I thought we should begin with these articles to understand the basics. We need to understand the circumstances in which Jesus operated. He did not manufacture and market products. He promoted a concept. We will take a look at how he did things. Let me call out a few lines from Mahatma Gandhi: *'Of all things I have read what remained with me forever, was that Jesus came almost to give a new law – not an eye for an eye but to receive two blows when only one was given, and to go two miles when they were asked to go one. It is the sermon that endeared Jesus to me.'*

"Gandhi, whom we respect, lived and died a Hindu, but he was not averse to reading the Gospels and getting to know Jesus. For those of us who have reservations on reading the Gospels, this thought should be comforting." He paused for a moment to let the idea sink in and continued: "Once you have read the material we could meet on Friday. Does that suit you?"

Lambert: "Friday morning is out. I am in the market. Friday afternoon should be okay with me."

The others had no words but nodded. The group disbanded after Joseph thanked them profusely for their time and participation.

As they returned to their desks, they found a copy of the New Testament and a note which read:

"You are shocked. Please do not feel guilty. I understand. We are professionals who do not fear to check options. Check this option, I implore you. If it is promising, we will pursue it. If not, we will drop it. Please find time to read the New Testament Gospels and the additional sheets. Knowing you, I can promise you one result – you'll enjoy it. Read the New Testament like you would read Stephen R. Covey or Tom Peters or your favorite management author. Disregard the religion in it. Do we consider the religious beliefs of Covey or Peters when we read them? We take in only the professional insights. In the same way, look for life-changing clues in the material I have given you. I am going to count on you doing just that. I am going to count on you ushering in change. May the best of your past, be the worst of your future!" Joseph.

Chapter Three: The Gospels

"When love and skill work together, expect a Masterpiece." C. Read.

Jesus was not keen on documenting his words and works. He even discouraged those who he healed from circulating information on their healing. The only reference to his act of writing is in John 8:6 - *"Jesus bent down and wrote with his finger on the ground."* Others wrote of him, his words and his actions. An authentic account is found in what is popularly called, The Gospels. Four writers put down facts and their commentary. There is much in common in their narratives, however, each is different in its own way. Mathew and John were two of his twelve disciples. Mark and Luke were followers of his disciples. Together the four have portrayed Jesus for all time. Long before Peter Drucker, Tom Peters, Stephen Covey, and others put down a game plan for managers, the Gospel writers uncovered the plan Jesus gave us.

MATHEW (28 chapters)

With Rome reigning over Palestine, tax collection was the extorting face of the emperor in the land he occupied. Tax collectors were his crafty emissaries who did his bidding. Mathew, one such tax collector, was seen as a stooge of the Rome. Like others in his trade, he was exploited by the Romans and despised by the Jews. Yet when Jesus, a Jew, called him, Mathew left everything and followed him to become a loyal disciple.

In his Gospel, he sets out to prove an audacious claim. Jesus Christ is the very Messiah, promised in the Old Testament. Christ is the Greek translation of the word Messiah. The Old Testament, as we know it, is an account of the lives, hopes, and travails of the Jewish people before the birth of Christ.

Epic stories in the Old Testament were lessons for the Jews. They listened to them often to affirm their faith in the coming of the Savior, foretold by many prophets. The Jews eagerly waited for the Messiah, the Promised One. They believed, his coming would change things. Could Jesus be the long-awaited Messiah?

Mathew starts with a genealogy to answer the question. Mathew does not begin with Christ's birth, instead, he reaches further back to establish his roots. He traces his lineage to the father of the Jewish race, Abraham. After recording Jesus' bloodline, Mathew narrates the story of his life on earth. He relies heavily on the Old Testament. Mathew frequently quoted from the Old Testament because he was writing mainly for the Jews.

What does a Tax collector like? Organized and neatly documented figures, accounting for all types of taxes. Mathew, the tax collector, turned disciple, did precisely that: organized thinking, in topically grouping facts.

First, in chapters 5-7, he inspires the reader through the famous Sermon on the Mount. Second, in chapter 10, he records the instructions Jesus gave his disciples on their mission. Third, in chapter 13, he lists a series of parables on the kingdom which Jesus tells his listeners. Fourth, in chapter 18, he records Jesus' words on the Church as a community. Fifth, in chapters 23-25, he describes Jesus' anger when he denounces hypocrisy. In the same chapters (23-25), he writes of the predictions Jesus makes on the future. The reader cannot but notice some order in his reporting. The reader also spots stories on money, natural to a tax collector.

Many important leaders work hard to convey an impression of confidence and power. A leader, they assume, should look like a leader, dress like one, behave like one, and project the image of one who is powerful. With the right image, he can attract crowds. In sharp contrast, Mathew depicts Jesus as the leader who broke stereotypes. He had power, enormous power, but he used power with compassion. He thought less of how others appraised him. Instead, he cared more for the needs of others and what he could do for them.

His leadership had many facets. One was distinctly seen as he neared the capital city of Jerusalem. He let the people take him through one moment of public triumph with wild cheering and exultation. Even in such a hero's welcome, he rode not a stallion, but a donkey colt. A few days later, he left his followers a lasting sign of shame and humiliation – the Cross, the sign of Roman punishment. Mathew shows how Jesus was composed in triumph and stoic in tribulation.

Jesus opened his ministry in his hometown, in a synagogue, a place of worship and discourse; an occasion that ended almost in a riot. When he returned to his hometown after visiting other towns, he aroused great curiosity, but little belief. The locals could not understand how, one raised in their town by a carpenter, could now teach them like a Rabbi. Some close to him even called him Master. How could this be? Mathew unravels the paradox deftly.

He recounts some of the growing tensions between Jesus and the groups that resisted him; they followed him from town to town, setting verbal traps for him. How did Jesus respond? Not by getting incensed, but by using the occasions of conflict to caution his disciples and the crowds who followed him, against the trickery of these troublemakers.

He was not trapped by their bait, instead, he had them hooked on their own line. Mathew 22:46 concludes: *"From that day, no one dared to ask him any more questions."* The Pharisees, the Scribes and the Sadducees, who were important sects, found in Jesus a formidable opponent. Continuing with the same theme in Chapter 23, Mathew records Jesus' eloquent verdict on the Pharisees. Jesus rebuked them for being proud and petty, and for refusing to admit their wrongs.

He went on to caution them that hypocrisy put distance between them and the common people. Mathew's Gospel depicts the multi-faceted personality of Jesus so well, the French skeptic Renan praised his Gospel as *"the most important book of Christendom – the most important that has ever been written."*

MARK (16 chapters)

Mark probably got his facts from Peter, the disciple of Jesus. And with those facts set about writing a fast-paced Gospel: clear, well-edited, with little scope for dialogue and reflection, but full of action. Adopting a rather unconventional style of writing, he records the impact of a historical figure, on his times. Jesus provoked strong reactions in everyone. He aroused fierce opposition among his own neighbors and among the religious die-hards. But the common people were amazed.

No Gospel writer describes the physical appearance of Jesus. Mark succeeds in painting a picture of his humanity: A very normal human being, compassionate to those in need, but angry at the hard-hearted response of his opposition. He was dismayed at the tricky questions that came from the suspicious religious leaders and troubled at their disbelief, although he excelled in repartee and logical debate. When he was weary, he wanted quiet and peace, away from the crowds. There were times he felt lonely and disappointed; and times when he was unashamed to weep over the sorrows of others.

Mark captures in words, a spectrum of human emotions that Jesus showed. Take this, for example, in chapter 12: in Jerusalem, Jesus is surrounded by hostile groups. Mark records a series of attempts made by the Pharisees, Sadducees, and others to trap him.

The intelligent and forthright manner in which he accepts and meets those challenges makes interesting reading – a case study in people management.

During much of his ministry, Jesus tried to dissuade people from praising his extraordinary powers and wondrous works. But in a rare scene, Mark depicts large crowds recognizing him as the Messiah and honoring him. In subsequent chapters, Mark recounts how the same crowds humiliate and disgrace him. He clearly demonstrates that public applause is short-lived. At the time of Jesus' death, the dramatic climax, Jerusalem is packed with people from all over the region. They are there for the Passover - a celebration of the time Jews was delivered from Egypt. Mark concludes that Jesus could not have chosen a better time to end his promising life. Like an experienced editor, Mark cuts and puts together pieces that read like an engrossing and exciting biography.

LUKE (24 chapters)

It is unlikely that Luke knew Jesus personally. But as a dedicated convert in the early Church, he accompanied the apostle Paul (who was not among the twelve disciples Jesus chose, but who joined the group after the death of the Master). In three of his letters, Paul refers to Luke with great affection.

Luke's Gospel is like a musical - a Greek Musical - composed by one who was hugely gifted. The mouth opens in a song when the heart is full of joy, and the tempo does not sag. In his introduction, Luke stresses the need to draw up a carefully researched account of Jesus' life and works. So, he gathers information from eyewitnesses. Scholars assume that he could have interviewed even Mary, mother of Jesus, to get his facts on the early life of her son. If Matthew's Gospel is one of teaching, Mark's Gospel, one of action, Luke's gospel is one of the relationships, which unfolds good character descriptions.

Among the Gospel writers, only Luke dated the events by referring to Roman Emperors. He was determined to write a thorough and factual account, which included dating events in their historical context. Mathew's gospel traced Jesus' roots back to Abraham, father of the Jewish race. But Luke, the only non-Jew writer of the gospels, emphasized that Jesus' good news was for all people, not just for the Jews. To prove that point he traced Jesus' lineage all the way to Adam.

Luke, a physician, knew first-hand about sick and suffering people. It explains the inclusion of physical healing and repeated reference to

Jesus' compassion for the afflicted. Luke shows him as a true servant of all humanity.

Jesus avoided such fashionable places as the resort town, Tiberias. He stayed near the farming communities and fishing villages around the Sea of Galilee, serving ordinary people. Different sections of people came to him. Each for a different reason: The sick, wanting healing; the hungry, hoping to be fed; the confused, seeking clarity; and even the rich and powerful, seeking blessings. He listened to each and empathized. Luke traces these encounters with rare diligence. Women, largely ignored by ancient historians, play a large role in Luke's gospel. He introduces thirteen women, not mentioned by other gospel writers; and he delights in including children in his narrative.

Jesus opposed the legalism and the blinkered views of some of the Jews. For example, some of them observed very strict rules governing the Sabbath. Jesus broke those rules. How? By helping people on the Sabbath, he explained to them that rules should not come in the way of assisting the needy. He refused to let traditions stop him from reaching out to those in distress. And what was the Jewish response? They were furious he flouted their edicts and would not rest until they hatched a plot to seize and kill him. They would not let even Pilate, the Roman Governor, foil the plot.

Luke, a master storyteller, records eighteen parables that appear nowhere else, even as he includes some of the more familiar. While Mathew emphasizes parables of the kingdom, Luke adds those that focus on people: The Good Samaritan, the Lost Coin, and the Prodigal Son are some.

In the parable of the Good Samaritan, the priest saw the waylaid victim in a half-dead state. According to the Old Testament Law, a priest who touched a dead body made himself unclean. Therefore, the priest and the religious Levite decided not to get involved.

The audience listening to the parable would have expected Jesus to introduce a third character, perhaps a Jew. But Jesus gave the story a twist. The third character, who stopped to help and show love, was not a Jew, but a Samaritan, a minority, despised by the Jews. In this parable, Jesus showed, the brotherhood of man did not recognize boundaries or limits; it embraced humankind.

Through his teachings and actions, Jesus showed how relationships could be built and sustained. Luke's gospel records those lessons.

JOHN (21 chapters)

John deviated sharply from the other three. They focused on events. He concentrated on the meaning of what Jesus said and did. John's Gospel is a result of great reflection. Using simple words Jesus conveyed great meaning. John's Gospel is full of those simple words that Jesus used eloquently.

Many specific details show that he was an eyewitness. He describes the stone water jars at Cana, where Jesus changed water into wine (2:6). He refers to Nicodemus who was a prominent Pharisee, a group violently opposed to Jesus. This Pharisee knew it was not prudent to meet Jesus during the day, so he chose to meet him at night and in secret (3:2). Two other remarks on Nicodemus show that Jesus had a strong influence on him. He stood up for Jesus at the Jewish Ruling Council (7:50) and helped prepare Jesus' body for his burial (19:39). Jesus' meeting with a Samaritan woman (4:4-42) probably had the same kind of intrigue as his forced encounter with the woman caught in adultery (8:3-11). A dialogue between a Jew and a Samaritan, let alone between a Rabbi and an adulteress, was taboo. Yet John highlights these encounters to emphasize Jesus' mission. He even records the exact number of fish caught by his disciples (21:11). John does not leave out the details which add to the credibility of his account.

The first six chapters he unfolds the identity of Jesus. The next six contrast the increasingly divided opinion on Jesus. On the one hand, his disciples were won over and Jesus gained a loyal following among the people. On the other hand, his enemies rejected all the evidence he presented. Ultimately their hatred spilled over and the venom was strong enough to kill. The remaining chapters fathom the depth of Jesus' words and actions. John omits many of the events recorded in Mark; many of the long speeches recorded in Mathew, and the parables of Luke. Instead John pictures close-ups of people who responded to Jesus: some who followed him openly; others who were suspicious; and some others who were hostile.

Although Mathew, Mark and Luke record miracles, John goes one step further to call them signs. A sign points to something. In John, supernatural acts are one more proof of Jesus' unique nature. Jesus refused to perform miracles as magic to dazzle the crowds but used them instead as object lessons.

That Jesus' life went even beyond what is recorded in the Gospels is clear in John 21:24-25: *"This is the disciple who is testifying to these things and has written them, and we know that his testimony is true. But there are also many other things Jesus did; if every one of them were written down, I suppose that the world itself could not contain the books that would be written."* A hyperbole all right, but the point is taken. There was more wonder in his life than recorded in the gospels; Jesus was too big to be confined to the pages of a text or caged between the covers of a book.

Through Mathew who highlights the public utterances of Jesus, Mark who unfolds his humanity, Luke who treats Jesus' relationships with sensitivity, and John who explains the meaning of His words and acts, we see the person of Jesus. In short, the Gospels provide an action plan for relationships and management. Jesus clearly establishes that his teachings can be practiced and that his people-management principles are for all time.

ACTS OF THE APOSTLES

This part follows the Gospels in the New Testament. It describes briefly the work of the disciples (now called apostles, messengers) after Jesus died and rose. It inspires the reader with the strong faith of the apostles in Jesus, and how his example powered them to phenomenal success – traveling to different parts of the world to spread his teachings.

* * *

On Wednesday, after supper, Richard withdrew into his study to read through this part of the articles that Joseph gave him. He connected the article with the book he recently read on the historicity of the Gospels – a book that he would recommend without hesitation to anyone in search of the truth: *A Case for Christ,* by Lee Strobel, published by Zondervan. He would bring it up with the others when he had a chance to discuss the articles. To interrupt his thoughts, Marion, his wife, walked into the study. He was glad she did and immediately began a discussion with her on what he had read. Her response was enthusiastic, as one who read verses from the Bible daily, and as a member of the Bible-Study Group in her parish. Her closing comment remained with her husband: *"When Jesus speaks it is final. There is no appeal against his words".*

Chapter Four: 2000 Years Ago

"Men build too many walls; and not enough bridges." D. Pire.

Some distance from Richard's apartment, in his well-furnished home, Sammy opened this article from the bundle of papers he held. He recalled his own studies in political science, where the history of events lent a new dimension to the subject. It was good to know the times Jesus lived in to understand his response. So thinking, he settled into his chair to focus on the reading material, as he sent a silent good wish to Joseph who gave him the papers. He decided to show Suman, his wife, the article. As a teacher of history in a local school, she would profit from the inputs.

* * *

The period in which we live is important because it impacts the way we think and act. Circumstances are significant and our responses to them are more significant. That is why a political leader is assessed against the turbulent times in which he leads his people; a corporation is gauged by the exacting conditions in which it operates, and a professional is appraised in the context of the tough environment in which he works. To understand the role that Jesus played and its relevance, it is necessary to examine the age and times in which he lived and worked – 2000 years ago.

Jesus was born in 4 B.C. in a stable in Bethlehem, an obscure village in Palestine. His mother was Jewish. He grew up like an ordinary Jewish child. Later, he worked as a carpenter, among Jews. When he turned 30, he started his public ministry among the Jewish people. For 3 years he went about this ministry with rare dedication. When he was 33, he was crucified and put to death by the Jews; the Romans were incidental. During his 33 years, he did not hold any public office, except being referred to as Rabbi – which is a teacher. He did not have a family of his own, or own a house, or have any possessions, but for the clothes he wore. He did not travel more than 200 miles from where he was born. He had no credentials but himself.

Such a sketchy reference to his life does him no justice. It does the four gospel writers no justice either. The purpose of the brief account is to stress his Jewish parameters. He was born a Jew, brought up as one, lived as one. He had to operate in Jewish conditions and cope with the contradictions the system bred. There seemed no escape. What were these Jewish conditions? Let us consider the Jewish race, to begin with.

THE JEWS

The Jews, as a people, were subjugated by the Romans. The yoke was heavy and the labor hard. Some chose to rebel and revolt, but most suffered in silence because they waited for a Messiah, the Promised One, who was foretold by the Prophets. This Promised One, the Messiah would liberate them from bondage, though such liberation was not prophesied. They believed he would come and trample the enemy underfoot, leading them to a long-awaited victory. So, there was hope and great expectation.

There were many groups. They spoke the same language (though in numerous dialects), believed in the same law and prophets and worshipped at the same temple, yet they were in a state of strife. Their strong rivalry paralyzed any joint effort against the Romans. Prominent among them were the **Pharisees** - the puritans of the day. They were law-enforcing, law-abiding custodians of the Law. They wore gaunt and hungry looks during a brief fast, prayed grandiosely if people watched and went so far as to strap verses from the law books on their left arms and foreheads. For them the letter of the law, and not the spirit, was important; the law given to them by Prophet Moses. The thought of foreign domination was revolting, yet they chose to be peaceful as long as the Romans did not interfere in their religious observances. They explained away the bondage as God-ordained.

The belief that the Messiah would come and deliver them, sustained them in difficult times. When he did come, he would dispense key positions to them in the new government; so, they hoped. Students of history have often puzzled over the friction between the Pharisees and Jesus. At first glance, he should have liked them because they openly professed their religious beliefs. Yet their over-legalistic behavior cast doubts on their motives, prompting Jesus to say: *"They do not practice what they teach."* Matt 23:3. The **Scribes** were a sub-sect of the Pharisees. They were the law experts. People in doubt went to them when they explained the law and clarified doubts. This was a vital function because the entire Jewish community was law-bound. The knowledge they had, conferred on the Scribes, a right to high positions in the Synagogue, the Sanhedrin and the Temple, important institutions of that time.

Despite their obsession with the Law, the Pharisees had the support of the common people, to fight another class known as the **Sadducees**. The Sadducees refused to accept the interpretation of the law given by the Scribes and Pharisees. For them only the first five books of the Old Testament – known as the Torah - were important; they disputed the other books. They were aristocrats, materialistic and politically well connected. They lobbied with the Romans to gain key positions.

The **Levites** were the priestly order, meant to hold priestly office. But, with the Sadducees occupying the top priestly positions, the Levites were relegated to lower levels in the hierarchy. The **Zealots** were a group of extremists. Barabbas, the criminal, whom Pilate offered as a trade-off for Jesus, was a Zealot. So were the criminals on crosses on either side of Jesus, when he was crucified at Calvary. The **Herodians** were a political sect pledged to support Herod, the King of Judea. Though a king, he too was subject to Rome. The **Publicans** were contractors engaged by the Romans to collect taxes. They were a hated group, because they collected more than was specified, and kept the difference. Matthew, the apostle, came from this group, as did Zacchaeus, the chief tax collector. The **Samaritans**, referred to in the parables, were social outcasts.

The Jews, by and large, had nothing to do with them. Anyone interacting with them was despised, including Jesus who tried to reach out to them. In all the groups, **women and children** hardly had a say. Men decided; women and children just obeyed. This ostracism in the decision-making process went so far as to forbid women from receiving religious instructions in the Torah, the five books of Moses. A Rabbi is known to have remarked, *"Rather should the words of the Torah be burnt, than entrusted to a woman."*

Jesus was concerned with the social oppression of women. He had very positive views on women and engaged them publicly in a discussion. The Samaritan woman at the well, Martha and Mary, and the woman who touched the hem of his garment, are some. Jesus understood the plight of widows, who were oppressed and helpless (Luke 7:12-13). In taking up the cause of women, he was strikingly original for his time. He offered a new way of relating that transcended divisions of rich and poor, slave and free, man and woman.

He proposed the making of a new community, one opposed to the enthroning of the individual or the exalting of any group. *"American culture encourages the individual to 'be all you can be'. Yet this extraordinary strength leaves America vulnerable because it ignores the needs of the larger community upon which even the strongest individual must depend. Individualism is only half of the solution."* - an extract from The Seven Cultures of Capitalism, by Charles Hampden Turner and Fons Trompenaars. Jesus anticipated and promoted this paradigm shift two thousand years ago.

THE INSTITUTIONS

The several Jewish groups in strife vied for honors in the celebrated institutions of that time - The Synagogue, The Sanhedrin, The Temple. The **Synagogue** was the Jewish place of worship and religious teaching. Prayers were offered, discourses were held, and doubts clarified in this holy place. It was in one such Synagogue that Jesus began his public ministry. After that, he frequently taught at synagogues.

The **Sanhedrin** was the highest Jewish court – the ruling council or assembly. It was made up of 70 (some experts place the number at 71) prominent citizens. The High Priest was the head of the Sanhedrin. The members belonged to 3 groups. The first was the Chief Priest group. They were prominent members drawn from families of former high priests and the current high priest. The second group, known as Ancients, comprised the wealthy and influential members of the laity. The third group came from the Scribes, the doctors of the law. Even though the Romans had conquered Palestine and a Roman government ruled the colony, the Jews were allowed to address many of their own problems. The Sanhedrin had the power to decide whether someone was innocent or guilty of breaking Jewish law. The temple Police enforced the verdicts of the Sanhedrin. But the council could not put to death a person found guilty, without the permission of the Roman Governor. That is why Pilate, the Roman Governor, had to be persuaded to pronounce the death sentence on Jesus. The Jews could only manipulate the situation to their advantage.

The **Temple** of Jerusalem, to the Jews of that time, was like Mecca to the Muslims of today – the holiest of holies. Even those who lived far away dreamed of a time when they would visit the temple and worship there. A good number made the visit once a year. Entry to the inner areas was restricted only to the Jews; transgressors were threatened with death. Women had limits marked out, beyond which they could not proceed. Because of the need for offering sacrifice – either for supplication or by way of penance – the sale of birds and sacrificial animals was brisk. Traders jostled to gain prime spots and moneychangers did good business. Such trading peaked at festival time, when hundreds of thousands converged on the temple. To cater to these worshippers' priests were necessary - at one time 24,000 of them were operating at the temple, vying for clientele and compensation. Although there was some division of labor among the priests, the more privileged functions were assigned to the high priests, who were Sadducees. The system automatically made them the head of the Sanhedrin. The clout they enjoyed was enormous. They could make or break careers and lives. With more and more people coming under the sway of Jesus' teaching, they feared that they would be side-lined. They could not let that happen and decided to break the stronghold Jesus had.

At Jesus' arrest, the religious and political leaders got a close look at him. They had heard of his miraculous powers and hoped he would perform for them like a magician. He had no such pact with them. Silently and firmly he declined. Not even with his life at stake would he humor them, bewitch them with miracles because he shunned the spectacular. He would use his powers only to help the needy.

The Gospels record a pass-the-buck sequence in Jesus' encounter with Jewish and Roman justice. The Sanhedrin judged Jesus guilty of blasphemy, but it did not have the authority to carry out the death sentence. They needed Pilate. So, they sent Jesus to Pilate. Along the way, they changed the religious charge against Jesus into a political charge of sedition, which alone would prompt the governor to take action. Pilate shunted Jesus to Herod, the king of Judea, who had jurisdiction over the home region of Jesus. Herod taunted and mocked Jesus, then sent him back to Pilate because he smelt a plot. Three times Pilate tried to release Jesus, but fear of offending Caesar, the Emperor, made him yield to the mob which was manipulated puppet-like, by vested interests.

LANGUAGE AND TRADE

Although Rome ruled, Greek influence was apparent. Next to Aramaic, a Hebrew dialect, Greek was the most widely used language. Luke wrote his gospel in Greek. It was also the language of commerce. And commerce was buoyant. Palestine, at that time, was among the more prosperous occupations in the Roman Empire. Wheat and Barley grew in abundance. Surplus grain went to Rome and to the other parts of the empire. Fruit, Olives, Figs, Dates, and Timber were traded in, and business thrived.

THE SABBATH

The Jews observed the Sabbath in the strictest manner possible. They almost deified the day. The day started at sunset on Friday and ended at sunset on Saturday. It was set aside for Divine worship. The best clothes were worn. The best food to eat (cooked, of course, the previous day). Physical work was restricted. The Sabbath day law listed many different physical activities that were prohibited. For example, walking beyond 3000 feet at a stretch was not allowed. Even the weight of articles to be lifted was specified. On the Sabbath, a man could ride a donkey. But if he used a whip to speed up the animal, he would be found guilty of laying a burden on it. Alms to a beggar could be given, on the Sabbath, only if he stuck his hand inside the home of the Pharisee, who would not have to extend his arm. A woman was forbidden from looking into the mirror. She might spot a grey hair and might be tempted to pluck it out – an activity that was ill-advised. The fanatical observances of the Sabbath were so extreme that the Jews refused to do battle on the Sabbath, even in the self-defense of their country. That gave the Romans reason not to recruit Jews into the Roman regiments stationed in Palestine.

The Jews had so sanctified the Sabbath with rules that it was no longer a day set aside for Divine worship. Instead, it became a day of stifling controls; a time when people, not adhering to the Sabbath Laws, would be penalized. Jesus admonished them: *"The Sabbath was made for humankind and not humankind for the Sabbath"* Mark 2:27. He declared that man was above the Sabbath and spurned their dictates on not helping the needy on the Sabbath. That he disdained petty observances, which they considered significant, roused their passions. They were being disregarded before their own people. Egos were hurt. And they would not take such an affront without retaliation.

THE LAW

At the age of six, the Jew was inducted into the knowledge and practice of the law. By the time he was an adult, he was fully indoctrinated. Sin, guilt, and atonement were impressed so deeply on his mind, that God was seen as a Judge who summarily punished the offender unless appeased through sacrifices. All activities were governed by the sacred books, so much so the Prophet Mohammed of Islam called Judaism *'the religion of the book'*. One such rule related to washing. The strict Jew had an obsessive fear of all kinds of pollution and had to continually wash as he laid down in the law. They faulted the apostles of Jesus who ate without washing their hands. Jesus typically responded: What goes into the mouth causes no offense, only malicious words that come out of it, hurt others.

Time and again, Jesus showed by example he not only respected the law, but also urged others to respect the law (Luke 17:14). He conformed to the ceremonial and judicial precepts of the old law. For example, when they asked for taxes, he told Peter to pay the tax demanded (Matt 17:27). Despite his willingness to honor the law of the land and pay his taxes, they hoped to trap him on that very issue. *"'Teacher, we know that you are sincere, and teach the way of God in accordance with truth and show deference to no one; for you do not regard people with partiality. Tell us then, what do you think. Is it lawful to pay taxes to the Emperor, or not?' But Jesus, aware of their malice, said, 'Why are you putting me to the test, you hypocrites? Show me the coin used for the tax.' And they brought him a Denarius. Then he said to them, 'Whose head is this, and whose title?' They answered, 'The Emperor's.' Then he said to them, 'Give therefore to the Emperor the things that are the Emperor's, and to God, the things that are God's.' When they heard this, they were amazed; and they left him and went away"* Matt 22:15-22.

Aware of their malice and with caution, Jesus replied their questions which were fraught with implications. If he said 'do not pay' he could be reported to the Emperor for rebellion. If he said 'pay', then the people who were rebelling against Rome would find a reason to distrust him. They thought he had no escape. He was trapped, back to the wall. They would watch him with glee, as he stood exposed. But Jesus was too much for them to handle. His pithy response had them running for cover. Smarting from defeat, they would wait to get even with him. (Luke 11:53-54).

They feared that Jesus was out to demolish the law, incapacitate them, and take control. They felt threatened not just by his great knowledge, the authority with which he spoke, but more importantly, by the response, he got from the people. But for the people, what would they have not done? *"Every day he was teaching in the Temple. The chief priests, the scribes, and the leaders of the people kept looking for a way to kill him; but they did not find anything they could do, for all the people were spellbound by what they heard."* Luke 19:47-48.

Despite their plots and threatening stance, Jesus allayed their fears when he reassured them that he had not come to abolish the Law but to fulfill it (Matt 5:17).

The fulfillment was meant to come about by giving the law a humane interpretation; a new justice; a new way of life. *"You have heard that it was said to those of ancient times, 'You shall not murder'; and 'Whoever murders shall be liable to judgment.' But I say to you that if you are angry with a brother or sister, you will be liable to judgment"* Matt 5:21-22. The new meaning was that hatred, which went before the murder needed therapy. Only then could the murder be stopped. By example he showed hatred cannot replace hatred. He visited the homes of the Pharisees, who hated him and supped with them in friendship. But Jesus did not hesitate to rebuke their hypocrisy (Mark 12:38). He faulted the deed, not the doer.

Unsuccessful in their attempts to do a verbal duel with him they changed tack and decided to foist false witnesses on him (Mark 14:55-56). Even then they failed because the witnesses would not corroborate the statements the accusers made. When they falsely accused him, his strong voice stayed silent. His silence was more eloquent than their vehement denunciation (Matt 27:12-14). Even Pilate who tried him was amazed at the way he conducted himself and sought to release him because he believed that Jesus was innocent. The law in its mangled form was sprouting tentacles to reach out and encircle Jesus. Those growing tentacles closed in on Calvary, the place of his crucifixion.

POLITICAL INTRIGUE

In this law-governed, faction-ridden, male-dominated society, the political situation was typically cloak and dagger. Each group huddled in a conspiracy to outwit the other. Vested interests defied the common good. Social climbers, religious pretenders, political heavyweights, used power and influence to have their way, as long as Rome was not ruffled. Like throwing a flaming torch onto dry grass, the situation threatened a raging fire.

THE ENVIRONMENT

In retrospect, what did the environment hold? A rather illiterate society presided over by people in power who crafted outcomes in different situations to suit their interests. The law was all-embracing. Traditions and rituals were not questioned. Rome was in control, aided of course by scheming and self-seeking Jews. Not that all Jews plotted. Often the problem is in the system. If you put good people in a bad system, you will get bad results.

Hope in the Liberator, the Messiah sustained many. But when he came, what a let-down it turned out to be! They wanted revenge and the overthrow of the oppressor. He preached forgiveness and reconciliation. They feared the men in power who wanted to perpetuate the law, if nothing else, to hold sway over the masses. He exposed contradictions in the law and offered them a new order; a radical change, nothing short of unlocking the person trapped deep inside. The liberated person would be free of pretense, rid of double standards, shorn of duplicity, and far removed from money-craze.

As a result of his new creed, the groups were split down the middle into those who believed in him and those who refused to believe even what they saw. Against the might of the Roman Empire and the Jewish power brokers, what could 13 (Jesus and his twelve disciples) men do? How would Jesus manage his meager resources? How would he establish his new order? Did he stand a chance in this environment? His short life had all the answers.

* * *

Setting the papers aside, Sammy wondered how complex things were for Jesus when he arrived on the scene. His task was daunting.

Chapter Five: Jesus - Fully Human and Fully Professional

"Goodness in words creates trust, goodness in thinking creates depth; goodness in giving creates love." Lao Tzu.

Lissy tucked Augustus into bed, finished odd jobs in the kitchen and wandered in to the living room of her commodious home. She found her husband flipping pages of his Bible.
"What are you doing?" she asked. Lambert had read the Bible a few times, thanks to his mother, but his memory needed refreshing.
"I am trying to catch up with what I read some time ago," he responded.
"Why? What is happening?" she continued.
To bring her into the loop, Lambert narrated all that happened with Joseph and his team of VP's. "We are to read the Gospels and some related material. I have finished two of the articles, and I'm getting ready to start on the third," he added.
"How can I help?" she asked.
"Perhaps you could read it to me, as I listen," he suggested. Pulling up a chair, Lissy sat down to read.

* * *

A certain company was going downhill. Morale was low, and key personnel left, afraid that things would continue to deteriorate. The chief executive, who had taken over only a month ago, was disturbed at the drift in the value system of his top team.
He decided to challenge his team to change. Ending an emotional address to them he said: "We are first and foremost human beings, then either husbands or wives, fathers or mothers, sons or daughters - and then we are professionals."

He reminded them professional priorities need not run counter to human values. Being a good professional is perfectly consistent with being a good person. With broad brushstrokes, he painted a picture of the model each should follow so that company operations, as a whole, would be the result of performance by enlightened professionals, of value-based actions.

Jack Welch put it in different words: *"Objectives and strategies don't get you there, values do."* And, advice from Stephen R Covey makes sense: *"For solutions during chaotic times, base it first on principles."* Are they the values and principles Jesus taught? There is a good reason to believe they are.

If one were to imagine Jesus in the place of that chief executive, addressing those professionals, would he have had anything different to say? Not likely. The message would have been much the same but, he would have stories to tell, embellished with figures of speech and crisp conclusions. His words would hum like tuning forks and his listeners would be astounded. "We are first and foremost human beings," he would affirm.

What would his words imply? As humans, we are part of a huge network from which we cannot break free. Why? Since the fatherhood of God is a given, we must accept the brotherhood of humankind - this relationship makes us unique. Invisible cords bind us, and those bonds get stronger with conscious help from within us. Was Jesus part of this network? Did he have a stake in building relationships with the people of his time? Did he have to struggle like us? Shall we check the facts?

1) **HUMAN**

a) Human Traits: *"He was a man like you and me,"* is how Kahlil Gibran referred to Jesus. As humans we think, feel and express our needs. We like and dislike, love and hate, judge and misjudge, and experience pain and pleasure. The package makes the person, not just one trait. Let us look for common qualities in Jesus and us.

As a normal human being, he experienced hunger (Luke 4:2) and thirst (John 19:28) and therefore ate and drank (Matt 9:10). He felt tired (John 4:5) and slept (Luke 8:23). Jesus also expressed a wide range of human emotions. He was filled with joy (Luke 10:21), surprise (Mark 6:6), compassion (Luke 7:13) and disappointment (Luke 17:17). He embraced children (Mark 10:16) and empathized with suffering women (Luke 7:13). He wept for his friend Lazarus (John 11:35). He needed human company and support like any of us (Matt 26:38) but, there were times when he wanted to be left alone, even as we do (Matt 14:13). Sometimes he grew impatient with the foibles of his disciples and admonished them (Matt 17:17). In changing circumstances, he changed his mind, as we do (John 7:8-10). When he found people hard-hearted and without mercy, he was angry (Mark 3:4-5). He became indignant when he saw the Temple desecrated. He drove out the money changers and those who were selling sacrificial animals (Matt 21:12-13).

In Jesus' day, activities at the Temple had taken on a commercial cast. Merchants sold sacrificial animals to pilgrims and foreigners at inflated prices. To visitors who paid in a different currency, money changers did not offer the correct rate of exchange and extracted an exorbitant fee. The system was designed more for a profit than as an aid to worship, with a nexus between traders and the temple management. Justly indignant, Jesus responded by chasing out these defrauders. Then he turned his attention to those in real need.

Was he afraid of rejection? Like any of us, he was, and John writes about it: *"Because of this* (teaching) *many of his disciples* (not the twelve) *turned back and no longer went about with him. So, Jesus asked the twelve, 'Do you also wish to go away?'"* John 6:66-67. The pathos in his words is palpable. Would the twelve reject him like the others? They were the closest and rejection by them would leave him friendless. Jesus would feel abandoned if they left. When those in his neighborhood and in his own town cold-shouldered him, he manfully coped with the affront, conceding prophets do not find honor among their own, and in their hometown (Mark 6:5).

Knowing different responses came from different segments, he wanted to know how people really saw him (Matt 16:13). When the disciples told him, that the general perception was that he was a prophet, he persisted (Matt 16:15), wanting to be told who they thought he was. Peter, speaking for himself and the others, answered his question fittingly: *He was Christ.*

Towards the end of his public ministry, when suffering and death were imminent, he was deeply distressed and weighed down, recoiling at the very thought of excruciating pain and abject humiliation (Mark 14:13). He hoped to be comforted by his disciples. The spirit was willing, not the flesh. They slept, and he felt forsaken.

Physically, he was very fit and strong. For several years he worked long hours as a carpenter, which gave him strong limbs and stamina. The punishment he took for many hours at the brutal hands of soldiers during his arrest and crucifixion was proof enough of his physical endurance.

A lesser mortal would have collapsed and died before getting to Calvary, the hill where he was crucified. A picture emerges of a person like us, sharing flesh and blood, mind and memory, reason and emotion, likes and dislikes, and normal human responses.

He was born to a young Jewish woman, descended from King David. She had no pretensions to fame or wealth. He grew up in a small artisan's family, respecting social customs and religious practices of the time. He would have easily passed for the good kid across the street, because of his obedient conduct. When he came of age, as expected, he learned a trade. Like a normal human, he grew in age and wisdom (Luke 2:52), which meant a stage-wise development as a man.

b) Intelligence: Even a cursory reading of the gospels gives us evidence of Jesus' intelligence. The speed with which he understood tricky questions put to him, the ready response he gave his adversaries, the ease with which he related to everyday human situations, the sharp comprehension he showed of puzzling matters, and the ability to read even the dark thoughts of those who challenged him (Mt.9:4), point to a well-developed intelligence. He could separate fact from fiction, the relevant from the trivial and the momentous from the minor. In an intelligence quotient (IQ) test he would have scored remarkably well.

What of his emotional quotient (EQ)? Is it different from IQ? Emotional intelligence (as explained by Daniel Goleman), measured in terms of emotional quotient (EQ), is the ability to acquire and apply knowledge about one's emotions and the emotions of others, to ensure problems are solved more successfully. Emotional intelligence is reflected in one's self-awareness, self-management, self-control, social awareness, and social skills, all of which lead to the building of better relationships. It is about ways that influence others to give of their best. EQ gives one the advantage of reading non-verbal signals in facial and body movements and tone of voice. The ability to understand what is said and what is not said. This skill is crucial since studies show 55% of communication is non-verbal. Despite these advantages, we tend to trust the information provided by the intellect more than vibes from emotion. Even the term *'emotional'* does not appeal to reason. It is viewed as a weak, out of control, and childish response.

The facts are different. EQ is more significant than IQ in successful people. Though some are academically brilliant, they are not as successful as they should be, because they lack the ability to socially interact and get the best out of others. They preen their own feathers and not stroke the feathers of others. With good reason, the corporate world is shifting emphasis from IQ to EQ.

How did Jesus measure on the EQ scale? He was aware of his extraordinary talents and used them wisely. Not to flash them before admiring eyes, but only to succor the needy. He checked his impulses to retaliate. Instead, he forgave. He showed no temper tantrums. Instead, he remained unruffled under provocation. Jesus was not rigid, but flexible in dealing with people. There are many examples of his social consciousness, his empathy, and his willingness to get involved in the social problems of his time.

The Gospels record many situations where the non-verbal skills of the Master made the listener feel good. Jesus looked into the face of the person he was speaking with, touched those he healed, ate among the crowds, sat among them when the group was small, stood in their midst when the gathering was large and always adapted to the situation, not losing the common touch. His non-verbal messages gave added meaning to his communication. His IQ and his EQ were exceptionally high. The combination was synergetic.

Danah Zohar and Ian Marshall, in their book, *"Connecting with our Spiritual Intelligence"*, assert that there is another important Q to consider – spiritual intelligence, expressed as a spiritual quotient (SQ). Spiritual Intelligence, the authors explain, is the ultimate intelligence with which we address and solve problems of importance; the intelligence with which we can place our actions and our lives in a wider and meaningful context; the intelligence with which we can assess that one way of acting is better than another. The authors stress SQ is the necessary foundation for both IQ and EQ. They defend their thinking that ethical living and spirituality are not things of the past, but essential today. Can we question the SQ of Jesus, when the Gospels are a revelation of his spiritual intelligence?

As one who walked with his people, experienced what they experienced, suffered what they suffered, he knew from the inside, as it were, the possibilities and the limitations of being human. In his humanness, he resonated with the deepest and best in us. And to confirm his humanness, he called himself *'The Son of Man'*. Dorothy Sanders, summing up his human traits, writes in Christian Letters to a Post-Christian World: *"He has himself gone through the whole human experience, from the trivial irritations of family life and the cramping restrictions of hard work, and the lack of money, to the worst horrors of pain and humiliation, defeat, despair, and death"*.

As a human, he operated in very human situations. In those situations, how did he manifest his beliefs and attitudes, knowledge, skills and work habits? Did he have skills of a high order? Did he have a style of his own? What was his profile? How different was it from those we know? We could begin by trying to understand what he considered as his mission.

2) **MISSION**

a) The Good News: In his words, proclaiming the good news, the new creed, the changed order, was important. That was his magnificent obsession. *"I must proclaim the good news of the kingdom of God to the other cities also; for I was sent for this purpose."* Luke 4:43.

What was the good news? It was the oxygen of life – Love; love of God and love of fellowmen. Love is something we do; the giving of ourselves; the sacrifices we make, even for people who offend us, or do not love us in return. It is an act of will and not feeling, though the feeling may accompany the act of will. Love is a value that is actualized through loving action. In a concrete way, Jesus was both the message and the messenger.

What did he mean by *'the kingdom of God?'* Mathew uses the term 30 times, Luke 31 times and Mark 14 times. Obviously, the power-packed expression conveyed more than the words. Some experts suggest he referred to a liberated communion of subjects, in the kingdom, building transformed and lasting relationships, instead of the bondage ordinarily seen in human affairs. His logic was simple, when we learn to love others, our relationship with them improves. Ties with others will be redefined, and because of a new way of looking at our relationships, we will be empowered.

Since his mission was so vital, he prepared himself through prayer, meditation, and fasting (Matt 4:2), before he started preaching and teaching. Aren't we reminded of how zealously and intensely we, humans like him, prepare when we undertake a major project?

b) Serving fellowmen: As an extension to proclaiming and teaching the good news, he also came to serve his fellowmen (Luke 22:27).
This was the second dimension to his mission, which he expressed lucidly when he said: *"You know, the rulers of the Gentiles (non-Jews) laud it over them, and their great ones are tyrants over them. It will not be so among you, but whoever wishes to be great among you must be your servant, and whoever wishes to be first among you must be your slave; just as the Son of man came not to be served but to serve."* Matt 20:25-28. By washing the feet of his disciples, at the last supper before his death, he set a lasting example of what he meant by serving others. By healing Jew, Roman, Greek and Samaritan, he showed he was not held back by boundaries.

c) Calling wrong doers to repentance: The third dimension to his mission was to call sinners to repentant. This is a goal that he articulates clearly to leave no one in doubt. Jesus answered: *I have come to call not the righteous but the sinners to repentance."* Luke 5:32.

To explain the point, he asks a valid question, using a situation his listeners could relate to: *"Which of you, having a hundred sheep and losing one of them, does not leave the ninety-nine in the wilderness and go after the one that is lost until he finds it? When he has found it, he lays it on his shoulders and rejoices."* Luke 15: 3-5. Going after the errant, to him, was a serious business. In the parables of The Prodigal Son (Luke 15:11-32) and The Lost Coin (Luke 15: 8-10), he reinforces this message.

LIVING HIS MISSION

How did he carry out his mission? By proclaiming the good news of love, serving his fellowmen and reaching out to sinners. Discern how one-part flows into the next. If one had love of God and love of one's neighbor (the first part), serving one's neighbor would follow (the second part); and if one loved and served one's fellowman, one would be concerned over his drifting away and try to bring him back on course (the third part). The three parts mixed like waters - easily.

Against such a lofty mission how did Jesus perform?
a) The Gospels are packed with passages that recount his teachings on the Kingdom of God, the **good news**. The Gospels also narrate how he trained his disciples to carry on the good work. The crowds he attracted, the discourses he held, the challenges he faced from his adversaries, which he converted into opportunities, all give ample evidence of his continuing attempts to put across the over-powering message of love: Love of God and love of one's neighbor. His frequent references to God, and his eagerness to do His will, state beyond any doubt his overwhelming love of God (John 14:31).

b) But what of his love for his fellowmen; how did he perform; did he **serve** his fellowmen as effectively as he declared? Here again, the Gospels recount many situations when his compassion overflows. His empathy is seen in acts of succoring the needy – those who lived on the fringes of society. The emphasis here is not on his remarkable performance, but on his willingness to help those in distress. It was not for acclaim or glory, but for the love of his fellowmen.

c) **What about wrongdoers?** They kept his company and he did not shun them (Matt 9:10). His unusual behavior was denounced by the Jewish Elders who condemned wrongdoers. Because Jesus did not follow their line, they tried to trap him. Consider the classic case: *"The Scribes and the Pharisees brought a woman who had been caught in adultery: and making her stand before all of them, they said to him*

'Teacher, this woman was caught in the very act of committing adultery. Now in the law, Moses commanded us to stone such a woman. Now, what do you say?' They said this is to test him so they might have some charge to bring against him. Jesus bent down and wrote with his finger. When they kept on questioning him, he straightened up and said to them, 'Let anyone among you who is without sin be the first to throw a stone at her.' And once again he bent down and wrote on the ground. When they heard it, they went away, one by one, beginning with the elders; and Jesus was left alone with the woman standing in front of him. Jesus straightened up and said to her, 'Woman, where are they? Has no one condemned you?' She said, 'No one, Sir.' And Jesus said 'Neither do I condemn you. Go your way, and from now on do not sin again.'" John 8:3-11.

Perhaps, this encounter has no parallel in the Gospels for suspense and tension. Swift action swirls around Jesus, even as he stays calm. The Pharisees and the Scribes are waiting to pounce on him. The sinner herself has lost hope. Jesus remains unruffled, although the man involved in the adulterous act was not brought to him for justice. In a male-dominated society, this was the typical cover-up for the man. After much questioning, Jesus decides to speak. The woman's accusers are sure of snaring him. They think, he has no escape. The law is clear. The evidence is conclusive. He must condemn her. But what does he do? He does not act as a Judge. He makes no accusations. He delivers no sermon. He stands on the law, which was their plank. Jewish law specifies two innocent witnesses are to throw the first stones. *'Who among you is sinless?'* he asks, without pointing an accusing finger. In one deft stroke, he demolishes their argument and exposes their hypocrisy. The tables are turned. The accusers become the accused. They know he has seen through their dark motives. They move away quietly and in disgrace.

He bends down to write, so they may flee unnoticed. They are vanquished but, there is no celebration. Only quiet reflection, as he bends down to write again. The woman expected no mercy from the crowds or from Jesus. She is surprised at the turn of events. Instead of condemnation, she receives forgiveness. Instead of punishment and death, she receives an acquittal. What better way to illustrate his lesson? What better way to win her over to repentance? Later, he gently persuades the woman to change her sinful ways. The Indian Poet, Thiruvalluvar, sang: *"The best way to punish the wrongdoer is to shame him/her by doing something good to him/her in return."* Could there be a greater good than calling him/her to repentance? More examples can be cited from the Gospels. The one we have just read is overpowering.

A TREE IS KNOWN BY ITS FRUIT

What we find is that Jesus performed creditably in all three areas of his Mission. His own performance only reinforced his strong belief that performance mattered, for anyone, in any function.

The slave in the parable he told, who did well by doubling the money entrusted to him, was not only complimented but also suitably rewarded. *"His master said to him: Well done, good and trustworthy slave: you have been trustworthy in a few things, I will put you in charge of many things; enter into the joy of your master"* Matt 25:21. As expected, the non–performing slave in the same parable, who did not use the money wisely, is reproached. Lucidly he summed up his thinking on non–performance when he said: *"Every tree that does not bear good fruit is cut down and thrown into the fire."* Matt 7:19.

His mission took up all of his waking hours, giving his work a sense of urgency. Luke 12:50 makes that clear. Much was to be done, and there was little time. His goal was to have his teaching reach the far corners of the world. He predicted it would come to pass (Mark 14:9). His disciples saw to it. The Acts of the Apostles, the part following the four Gospels in the Bible, is a stirring account of how the disciples set about spreading Jesus' message to different parts of the world.

3) BELIEFS

a)The Golden Rule: His strong beliefs gave his mission direction and momentum. At the top of the list of his beliefs is the Golden Rule: *"In everything, do to others as you would have them do to you."* Matt 7: 12. Put simply, there is no room for double standards, which is following one rule for me and enforcing another for you. That is how we normally transact. No. That is not the way it should be, he entreats. Condensing many of his teachings, he declares that the Golden rule embodies the secrets of good relationships – value others as you value yourself.

Over the centuries, the world has agonized over this dictum. How can we treat others as we want to be treated? That is preposterous, the world argues. Self must precede others, it demands. That is why Law and Justice, distant cousins, are not on speaking terms. In delivering Justice, selfish variables intervene to distort a straight case that Law makes out. Translating Law into unbiased judgment is never easy, double standards will not give way. This shocking distortion was seen at Jesus' trial. Pilate was convinced Jesus was innocent because his detractors could not prove their accusations. Law and Justice could have met on friendly terms, but Pilate's strategy was to play it safe, to protect his interests. He did not want to be seen as offending the Roman Emperor. The Jews falsely accused Jesus of aspiring to become King. Pilate's selfishness and ambition played foul to thwart Justice. He knew he would face no problem crucifying Jesus, who had no links with the Emperor. He did not value justice as much as he valued his position. Pilate failed the test. We, as professionals, also fail many times when we compromise the truth and put self over others and fair play.

The Golden Rule (Matt 7:12) is resented time and again because it calls us to rise above double standards, to disown foul play and to uphold fair play. Jesus' words test our sincerity, our thoughts, our words, and our deeds. They nudge us to honor fair play. Give others what is due to them, be both unbiased and just. His words also apply to the choice we have to make between serving self and serving others. He does not suggest exclusion of self, but an inclusive behavior which embraces others as well. We recall, he advocates love for others as strongly as he encourages the love of ourselves. It follows, love for self is not against his teachings, but a part of it. With God, as the Father, whom we love, we are bonded with others inseparably.

It is true, some other great thinkers also spoke and wrote of the Golden Rule (Example, the Jewish Talmud: *"What is hurtful to yourself, do not do to your fellowmen")*. Why then does Jesus' teaching on the Golden Rule stand out? For two reasons: First, Jesus spoke with authority; the others offered a suggestion they tried to formulate into a lesson. They were men with feet of clay – like many of us, they erred. In sharp contrast, there was no dichotomy in the way Jesus spoke and acted – upholding the truth in all circumstances. Even his critics and adversaries could not accuse Jesus of wrongdoing. He was blameless. That is why his character towers over the others who also proposed the Golden Rule. Second, Jesus does not express the Golden Rule in a negative manner (For example: *"What you do not want to be done to yourself, do not do to others."* Confucius). It is easier to avoid doing evil to others than to take the initiative and do good. The Golden Rule, as Jesus taught it, is the foundation of active goodness and mercy. It is fundamental to building good and solid relationships.

b) **One cannot serve two masters:** He vividly stated another of his beliefs: *"No slave can serve two masters; for a slave will either hate the one and love the other or be devoted to the one and despise the other."* Luke16: 13. We cannot choose good and evil at the same time. We must be careful with our hard choices. These choices might not be related to persons (masters), but deities we install and worship, anything to which we get enslaved. For example, one cannot go after Fame and Modesty (two very different masters), at the same time. It is a contradiction. The pursuit of fame tends to make one, *'puffed up'*, in the words of St. Paul. Jesus implies we have to reconcile our goals in life to bring order into our minds and set our priorities right. When our priorities are not right, we give the less important things in our life more attention and the more important things less attention. That is when results are far from satisfactory.

c) **To be wise:** In our transactions with others, Jesus does not condone naivety and foolishness. In a parable of practical dimensions, he tells of five prudent virgins, who pour enough oil in their lamps and of five naive and foolish virgins who do not fill their lamps with enough oil, to join the bridegroom's procession with lighted lamps. When the bridegroom arrives, the wise virgins join the procession and attend the banquet (a practice popular at the time), but the foolish ones are shut out (Matt.25:1-13). Foolish behavior has no excuse. Without reserve, he commends the wise (Matt 10:16) and advocates alertness and foresight (Luke 12:35). Such wisdom, he says, will surely find expression in shrewd common sense. He cites two situations to make the point: *"For which of you, intending to build a tower does not first sit down and estimate the cost to see whether he had enough to complete it?"* Luke14: 28. And, *"what king, going out to wage war against another king, will not sit down first and consider whether he is able with ten thousand to oppose the one who comes against him with twenty thousand?"* Luke 14: 31. Shrewd Common sense is the canopy across all his teachings and actions. Holding up the canopy of common sense are two stalwarts - **Honesty and Fidelity.**

He exalts them when he says: *"Whoever is faithful in a very little is faithful also in much, and whoever is dishonest in a very little is dishonest also in much."* Luke 16: 10. Honesty and fidelity are not minor, but major virtues, he stresses. Having them makes sense when transacting with others because, without them, we compromise our relationships.

d) **Attachment to wealth:** Does honesty have a bearing on a man's attitude to material possessions, to wealth? Is an unbecoming attachment to material acquisitions approved? Jesus has very definite ideas on such attachment (Luke 12:23). In a world that is wealth-starved, his words are not food for such hunger. *"Take care! Be on your guard against all kinds of greed; for one's life does not consist in the abundance of possessions."* Luke 12: 15. It cannot be denied that greed tests honesty and avarice lead to compromise. To prove the point, he made no exceptions. Speaking of himself, he said he had nowhere to lay his head. He had no place to call home (Matt 8:20). He had no possessions to call his own and no money. But he is practical. He is not against money. Money has its use. It is necessary. What he is against is an obsessive attachment to money since it warps values. St. Paul conveyed the master's thinking lucidly, *"For the love of money is the root of all kinds of evil,* "1 Timothy 6:10. Money is not the root of all evil, but the excessive love of money.

S. K. Chakraborty and Pradip Bhattacharya, in their book, Human Values – "The Tagorean Panorama", explain briefly why attachment to wealth is obstructive, *"Christ had said, just as it is impossible for a camel to pass through the eye of a needle, so it is impossible for a rich man to attain salvation. The meaning is: --he, too, because of his increasing grossness* (attachments), *cannot make his way into the universal".*

* * *

"Please read that paragraph again. I remember reading a book on human values," Lambert interjected, and Lissy obliged. Lambert pondered those words for a moment; then he signaled for her to continue reading.

* * *

In a parable, Jesus puts things in perspective: *"A man planted a vineyard, and leased it to tenants, and went to another country for a long time. When the season came, he sent a slave to the tenants in order that they might give him his share of the produce of the vineyard."* Luke 20:9-10. We have a right to our share of the produce; to our share of profit. No one can take away that right. Profit is not a dirty word. Money is not obscene. Work must be rewarded. In the case of the laborer, he is very specific: *"For laborers deserve their food,"* Matt 10:10, and their wages too. Stephen R Covey echoes these statements when he exhorts us to make money for noble reasons. For example, for the family but he advises against money becoming the center. Such attachment, he warns, could bring about one's undoing. Covey adds, at best, with money, we could buy people's hands and backs, but not their hearts and brains or their loyalty and creativity.

e) **Responding to enemies:** When we are not attached to wealth or possessions and we are fair to others, we believe there will be no discord. Fair conduct does not insulate us from all dangers. Enemies sprout, almost from nowhere, through envy or jealousy, sadism, or sheer cussedness. How are we to handle such enemies? *"I say to you, love your enemies."* Matt 5: 44. The advice Jesus gives is difficult to follow, almost impossible, we may contend. Jesus takes it further: *"But if anyone strikes you on the right cheek, turn the other also."* Matt 5: 39. Jesus' words, in today's context, have bothered many people. We can understand them better when we remember the custom in Jesus' day was to give a light left-handed slap on the face of an adversary to show disdain for him. This was not meant to be a painful blow, but an insult. Jesus must have startled his listeners when he suggested offering the other cheek. He was not suggesting that force must never be used to restrain evil. In whipping fraudsters at the Temple, Jesus proved that evil must be fought. Rather, he was saying, by offering the other cheek, we reject the spirit of retaliation towards those who offend us. Instead, we offer them forgiveness.

There are some critics who insist he should have practiced what he preached when the soldier struck him after his arrest. Why did he not turn the other cheek? Instead, he questions the soldier (John 18:23). They conclude, there is a contradiction. Again, he questions the crowd who want to stone him (John 10:31-32). Here too, the critics are emphatic there is a contradiction. To resolve these contradictions, we shall have to go back to the Golden Rule (Matt 7:12).

What he meant was: Love your neighbor as much as you love yourself. Love of self is important; it is not taboo. Only if we love ourselves, can we love our neighbor. We cannot let ourselves be exploited or abused, without protest. Jesus showed, by prudent action, one has a right to love and protect oneself. *"So, from that day on, they planned to put him to death. Jesus therefore no longer walked about openly among the Jews but went from there to a town called Ephraim in the region near the wilderness, and he remained there with his disciples."* John 11:53-54. By staying clear of his enemies, he showed no bravado, just sensible behavior. If protecting oneself is important and right, Jesus did no wrong in defending himself against unjust soldiers or a frenzied mob. There was another compelling reason: he had yet to complete his mission, and more work had to be done. His time for Calvary had not yet come.

His maxim on the enemy must be seen in the context of the Jewish law which stated: *"An eye for an eye and a tooth for a tooth."* Matt 5:38. Retaliation was the law; give back in equal measure. Against that conditioning, to persuade the Jews to think differently was difficult. So, in different ways Jesus spoke of love and not retaliation. He was emphatic on forgiving offenders and not nursing grudges against them. He was also for confronting injustice and for protesting violence. Questioning soldiers and the crowd was not retaliation, but the questioning of injustice, in his case. He stood up for what was just, non-violently. As a human, he had his rights. Later, at the time of his arrest, Peter brandished a sword and cut off the ear of a soldier. Jesus admonished him, again establishing that friend or foe, one had to be fair; the soldier was only doing what he thought was his duty. (Matt 26:52). He would not condone tit-for-tat behavior from Peter, his disciple.

Still later, at his passion, he endured abject humiliation and excruciating pain without protest. His silence amazed his persecutors. He knew he could not reason with them. Pilate also knew the Chief Priests handed over Jesus out of jealousy, and not because he was guilty (Mark 15:10), but because his time for calvary had come.

f) **Truth**: Pilate was intrigued by the way Jesus conducted himself during the trial. When Jesus said that he had come to testify to the truth, Pilate asks a rhetorical question: *"What is truth?"* John 18:38. Pilate does not ask: *'What is the truth?'* Jesus did not answer the Governor because there was no room for words when he stood as testimony to truth.

On an earlier occasion, he called himself the truth. Truth in Greek philosophy is what is opposed to falsehood. In Hebrew thinking, Truth is more definite, suggestive of trustworthiness, steadfast love. Jesus personified truth – steadfast love in upholding and living the truth, in word and deed. That is why he confirmed that the truth set one free, while the opposite bound one in knots.

It does take some intent and effort to understand and resolve the apparent contradiction between his exhortation and example. In the end, Jesus stands vindicated. He showed no double standards. He lived his beliefs. Like reflections from a diamond that cannot be separated from the source, his beliefs were part of his enlightened Mission; inseparable.

4) **KNOWLEDGE**
The Gospels extol his superior knowledge of the Scriptures (The Old Testament) from where he frequently quoted. He engaged scribes and Pharisees in animated debates and resolved doubts raised by those in top positions. Even the Scribes who were the acclaimed experts, the doctors of the Law, were amazed at his understanding and his answers

(Luke 2:47)."*They were astounded by his teaching, for he taught them as one having authority, and not as the scribes.*" Mark 1:22. The crowds who heard him comprised the low, middle, and upper classes. Most of them were tutored in the Jewish Law and were acquainted with the Old Testament. So, for them to be '*astounded*' was making a statement on his knowledge and ability to communicate that knowledge.

To explain his teachings, Jesus referred to the work experience of builders, soldiers, doctors, teachers, tax collectors, farmers, traders, business managers, landowners, fisherfolk, shepherds and loan sharks. He was familiar with plowing of fields, sowing of seeds, harvesting, winnowing crops and storing produce in barns. He knew the relative merits of soil and the impact on crop yield. He talked on the vagaries of the weather. He spoke of the need to dispose of weeds wisely and to prune vines to increase fruit. He spoke of birds, trees, other vegetation, fish, insects, serpents, and animals. His personal experience as a carpenter gave him first-hand knowledge of timber, furniture and the building industry. He knew the joys and customs of happy occasions like weddings and the sorrows of sadness with death and funerals. He was aware of problems families faced, the plight of the marginalized, the hazards of life from the actions of lawless people, and the injustice the rich could unleash. People even approached him to resolve legal disputes.

TOTAL QUALITY MANAGEMENT

This passage was gleaned from several available: *"Then Jesus said to the disciples: There was a rich man who had a manager, and charges were brought to him that this man was squandering his property. So, he summoned him and said to him, 'What is this that I hear about you? Give me an accounting of your management, because you cannot be my manager any longer"* Luke 16:1-2. Notice the terms Jesus uses, 'Manager, Management, Accounting', everyday language in corporate circles. He also puts emphasis on proper management, where the manager is held accountable.

In business circles, there has been much talk on Total Quality Management – TQM. We could hazard a guess. TQM found favor with Jesus 2000 years ago. How? In simple terms, TQM is a way of transacting to help the company meet customer expectations and continually improve on the quality of such transactions. This implies customer focus. It means finding out what the customer expects and orienting the company to deliver it, making a profit in the process. So *'listen to the customer and respond'* is the axiom. Let us examine how Jesus went about listening and responding to his customers. Virtually everyone got a prompt response, with no condescension, only empathy. Their expectations were exceeded. They were delighted. Even his adversaries (the Scribes) had to grudgingly admit to their satisfaction, as Luke 20:39 points out: *"Then some of the scribes answered, 'Teacher, you have spoken well'."* John 7:45-46 refers to yet another compliment, *"Then the temple police went back to the Chief Priests and the Pharisees, who asked them, 'Why did you not arrest him?' The police answered, 'Never has anyone spoken like this'."* With Oliver Goldsmith, we could recite, *"Those who came to scoff remained to pray."* So forceful and complete was his response to his customers, the Pharisees then said to one another, in despair: *"You see you can do nothing. Look the world has gone after him!"* John 12:19. The competition was definitely worried. The CSI (Customer Satisfaction Index), if there was a way of measuring it then, would have been a chartbuster and a trend-setter

The TQM concept also extends to the internal Customer, the employees. Their satisfaction mattered. The assumption being, only a satisfied employee would try to satisfy the company's customers. If the disciples are regarded as employees (subordinates), their statements and actions will give us an idea of the Employee Satisfaction Index (ESI). When Jesus inquired if the twelve apostles would forsake him like some other disciples who refused to walk with him, Simon Peter, speaking for the team, said, *"Lord, to whom can we go?"* John 6: 68. They excluded all options; they were with him and that would not change. Perhaps the spontaneous tribute Thomas, the disciple, paid Jesus is unsurpassed: *"Let us also go, that we may die with him"* John 11:16. Peter's unreserved declaration adds credibility to Thomas' idea of solidarity with the Master, *"I will lay down my life for you"* John 13: 37; which he did. Jesus identified himself with his disciples, his team. In return, they gave him a massive mandate.

TQM also implies continuous improvement. In his ministry, Jesus set about continually improving the disposition of people. That is why some call him a Change Agent. Peter, the fisherman, turned disciple, denied Jesus three times, only to later lay down his life for him. Mathew, the tax collector, gave up his money craze, to become his disciple and stay faithful to him. After his encounter with Jesus, Zacchaeus, the chief tax collector who defrauded people, promised to make good four-fold to those he cheated. The woman caught in adultery, found forgiveness and acquittal. She would not have profited from the Jewish Law in the same way. The Samaritan woman at the well, who, at different times, had lived with five men, had a change of heart and invited the people of the town to meet Jesus and listen to his teachings. The Centurion, shedding his Roman ways, told Jesus only a word from him would be enough to heal his servant. Nicodemus, a highly placed Pharisee, went to Jesus to unlearn and learn. The crucified thief on his right, at Calvary, begged Jesus to remember him and rebuked his unrepentant fellow thief, who was hanging to the left of Jesus. Just a few names are listed here. In each case, Jesus brought about a transformation; as a change agent he redefined values and spotlighted the evil of attachment. He showed them how, kindness, compassion, honesty, respect, and generosity, would transform relationships. He showed them, very subtly, that conflict sprang from greed, lust, and hatred. Change was just a decision away.

The sign of a good Change Agent or Change Leader is the habit of abandoning yesterday and embracing today and tomorrow. Peter Drucker called this *'organized abandonment'*. Jesus did not dwell on the past. He placed before each person the present and the future: *'Go and do likewise, go and sin no more.'* It was always the future, never the past. He did not ask them: "Why did you sin yesterday?" or "Why did you behave badly yesterday?"

TQM aims at more profit from improved performance. So, if TQM found favor with Jesus, the question that follows is: what profit did Jesus earn? Jesus kept no accounts. To him, profit was the changed attitude, the reformed disposition, the new mindset of those he tried to transform. When that happened, he profited, and going by the many who changed, Jesus profited immensely. The bottom line looked healthy. If his company stocks were traded, the market would have turned bullish.

Edward Juran and Joseph Demming initiated and propagated quality concepts, culminating in TQM. Without taking credit away from them, we must assert Jesus operated on the same lines. Jesus didn't worry about labels, but concept and content. With his listeners, we may exclaim: *"How does this man have such learning!"* John 7: 15.

5) **SKILLS**

Now, let us consider the skills Jesus demonstrated. People were 'amazed' at his range of skills. His Team management skills, interpersonal skills, and communication skills made a great impact on people of his time. These skills call for separate and special treatment and therefore appear under separate chapters. Lessons for professionals will be drawn from these chapters.

6) **WORK HABITS**

He was not content camping in one place, waiting for his customers to come to him. Instead, he went out to them and worked long hours at his Mission. As Luke writes: *"Soon afterward he went on through cities and villages, proclaiming and bringing the good news of the kingdom of God"* Luke 8:1. He had only three years of public ministry and had to make the best use of each day. So he began early, as Mark 1:35 points out: *"In the morning, while it was still very dark, he got up and went out."*, And like all good leaders, he cultivated an eye for detail, even when planning his itinerary, as Mark 3:9 states.

Good professionals learn to use available resources effectively, not deriding paltry ones. On more than one occasion, we see him use his resources prudently, often improvising and advising his disciples to do likewise. Even when he multiplied five loaves of bread to feed five thousand people, he ensured the leftovers were collected in twelve baskets. There would be no waste; resources are precious.

As both a professional and a leader, his mission, beliefs, knowledge, skills and work habits fuse, to uncover a human of rare excellence. This outstanding professional, so to speak, walked like a colossus, leaving giant footprints.

* * *

Lissy finished reading and looked up at Lambert, who said: "Thank you, Lissy. You read well. I liked the way you intoned." Lissy smiled and touched him tenderly. They rose and went to bed; it was long past bedtime.

Chapter Six: Relationship with The Team

"The Leader must be everything that he desires his subordinates to become. Men think as their leaders think and most know unerringly how their leader thinks." General Summerall

On Thursday morning Anjali walked into Joseph's office to tell him she that would be visiting the bank to discuss a sizable loan for new product promotion, that Lambert had espoused. Joseph was pleased and asked her if she needed help from him. She said she would get back to him after her meeting with the bank. She was about to leave when Joseph asked, "How is the reading going?" She smiled and said she had read two of the articles and The Gospel of Matthew, adding she would squeeze out time during the day to read the next article – which she did after a hurried lunch.

* * *

Some leaders steal credit from their team-mates to appear big. They hog the limelight, belittling the contributions of their team members. The word *'tragic'* comes to mind when referring to such sorry specimens. Little do they realize that leaders cannot complete projects without the help of teams! The grand scheme is crippled without the right team. A leader with foresight selects a team to help him achieve team objectives. To get the best out of his team, he nurtures and values them. He assigns credit for their contributions and cradles them in compassion. It is obvious that leaders cannot demand a title, they must earn it!

In his essay, *"The Twelve Men"*, dealing with the British Jury system, G.K. Chesterton wrote: *"Whenever our civilization wants a library to be cataloged, or a solar system discovered, or any other trifle of this kind, it uses up its specialists. But when it wishes anything is done, which is really serious, it collects twelve of the ordinary men standing around. The same thing was done, if I remember right, by the founder of Christianity"*. Jesus Christ was into something serious. To spread messages born of his mission, he needed a team to assist him. He chose twelve ordinary men, who were known as his disciples. These twelve were given a mammoth task: *"You are the salt of the earth. You are the light of the world."* Matt. 5: 13-14. By their standards, they were given very ambitious tasks. Jesus did not stop at that; he raised the bar even higher, exhorting them to, *"Be perfect"* Matt 5: 48. That was the ultimate standard. He knew, even as he set those standards, that they were very ordinary, frail men. Attaining high standards would be almost impossible for them. Yet, to Jesus what mattered was the effort. The Japanese have a nice way of saying it, fall down seven times, but get up eight. Jesus conveyed the same message to his team. Do not give up trying.

What were the names of the twelve disciples? *"These are the names of the twelve Apostles, first, Simon, also known as Peter, and his brother Andrew. Next was James, son of Zebedee, and his brother John. Then, Philip and Bartholomew, Thomas and Mathew the tax collector. James, Son of Alphaeus, Thaddaeus, Simon the Cananaean, and Judas Iscariot, the one who betrayed him"* Matt 10: 2-4. Most of the disciples do not have detailed character descriptions in the Gospels. From the sketchy references to them, we find that Peter was spontaneous and impulsive. He often spoke for the rest, in a way demonstrating his leadership quality.

John, also known as the Beloved Apostle, was comparatively young and given to passionate outbursts. With his brother James, he jockeyed for the best positions. Mathew, the tax collector, was better educated but, he was despised because of the job he once held. Simon (the Cananaean) was a Zealot - the group given to violence and rioting. Andrew was sociable and open. His Greek friends are mentioned in the Gospels. He is seen as operating at his own pace, and as one willing to help his friend Philip - described as pure in spirit, simple and not given to manipulating others, and rather shy.

Jesus warmly compliments Bartholomew (Nathaniel) as one who has no deceit in him. Impetuous and generous to a fault is Thomas. Often referred to as *'Doubting Thomas'*, because he refused to believe that Jesus had risen from the dead. The Gospels are rather silent on James, son of Alphaeus and Thaddaeus. Judas (like Jesus) was a common name for Jewish men in those days. It is the Greek form of Judah. He came from a region called Judea, while the other disciples came from Galilee. Yet Judas Iscariot gained enough trust to be the treasurer of the team. He had political aspirations and hoped Jesus would help fulfill them.

What fanned his hopes for a time was the attempt by the people to force Jesus to become king. Not he alone, but the others also were impressed each time Jesus was acclaimed by the crowds.

They expected such ovations would build to a crescendo which would have political overtones. The Master did not seek public office, he had different objectives.

a) Choosing his team: How did Jesus go about choosing these men? The fact remained he chose them (John 6:70). The brief account of their selection is fascinating.

In a head-hunting exercise, he planted a seed in them. Then he let the seed germinate, *"As he walked by the sea of Galilee, he saw two brothers, Simon, who is called Peter, and Andrew his brother, casting a net into the sea - for they were fishermen. And he said to them, 'Follow me, and I will make you fish for people.'* Immediately they left their nets and followed him. As he went from there, he saw two other brothers, James, son of Zebedee and his brother John, in the boat with their father Zebedee, mending their nets, and he called them. Immediately they left the boat and their father and followed him" Matt 4:18-22.

We cannot help admiring the charisma of the man who called them to give up their all and follow him, almost in an act of total surrender. They showed no hesitation, only immediate compliance. They were prepared to break with their past and not stop to inquire about the compensation he would give them in return. They did not check on the kind of hardships they would have to endure. He called; that was all that mattered (Luke 5:11). It may be argued that they had very little to give up, which is true. It must not be forgotten that the little they had was all they had - their livelihood and their families.

Why did Jesus choose such men? Why did he choose such a motley crowd? Why not select others with better profiles? We do not have definite answers but, some assumptions are possible. Perhaps he found it easier to train and mold these simple people, rather than the I-know-it-all type. The twelve were prepared to unlearn and learn again. Another assumption is that Jesus had very few options. Most common people were illiterate. Of course, in the Gospels, we meet people in high positions. They had their attachments: to money, to possessions, to positions. They were not the right type to join a leader who moved, gypsy-like, from village to village and from town to town.

Mathew makes it clear, of the twelve, Simon Peter is first. Peter's name repeats 195 times in the New Testament. The names of all the others repeat 130 times. From the beginning, Peter was chosen to lead the rest. With him as the key figure, Jesus sought to establish an Inner Circle, a core group of Peter, James, and John (Mark 9:12); the other nine came next. He began with twelve, as the scale of operations widened, he expanded the size of his team. He appointed another seventy (Luke 10:1). In corporate parlance, one could say Jesus set up a flat structure. Twelve on the one side subtly separated into the inner circle of three and the remaining nine. On the other side was the more recently recruited group of 70. Although he dealt with the two groups directly, the new group of 70 sought the help of the 12 in transacting with the Master. A dotted line relationship is visualized. Although some others wished to join him, he was not eager to enlist more disciples into his team.

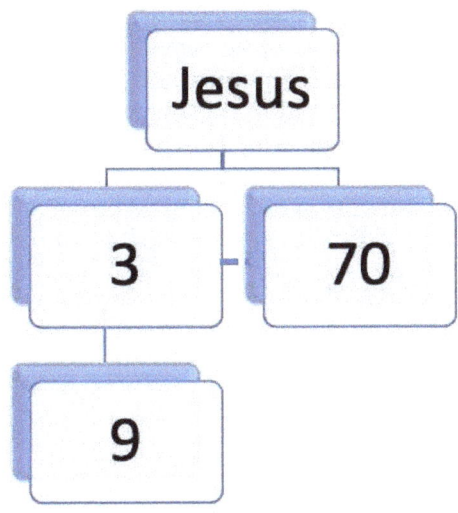

b) Managing a weak team: His team was as frail and disjointed as those we have in corporate circles today. They were ambitious and squabbled over favored positions (Luke 9:46). Even at the emotional last supper, they worried about rank and status. Despite Jesus' assurances (Matt 10:31), meant to dispel fear, they were a timid lot, anxious and stressed; who deserted him and fled when Judas and soldiers arrested him (Matt 26:56). They amply demonstrated the mixture of good and bad qualities present in most of us. Yet, unlike most of us, they were dense. With them some of the most obvious facts did not register; they understood little (Luke 18:34). Therefore, Jesus had to contend not just with their human infirmities, but also with their low level of understanding. It made his task all the more difficult. Like a good big brother (although he was younger than most of them) he took them into his huge embrace - warts and all - and called them his friends: *"I do not call you servants any longer, because the servant does not know what the master is doing; but I* *have called you friends because I have made known to you everything"* John15:50

c) Expecting obedience and commitment: What compensated their obvious weakness was their willingness to abide by the conditions Jesus laid down: *"If any want to become my followers, let them deny themselves, take up their cross and follow me"* Matt 16:24. A total commitment was the entrance fee to this exclusive club. They willingly paid the fee. Knowing Jesus valued their obedience, they readily complied (Matt 21:6). These faithful followers were always close to him. He spent most of the three years of his public ministry in their company. He grew to love them and treated them with great affection. They responded not out of duty, but because they loved him. No man had ever struck such a responsive chord in their hearts. He had stirred in them a dormant capacity to love, that even his commands were received through doors of love. St. Paul wrote of such a relationship in one of his letters, *"For this reason, though I am bold enough in Christ to command you to do your duty, yet I would rather appeal to you on the basis of love"* Paul to Philemon 8-9. Dag Hammarskjold, former UN Secretary-General, echoed the same thought: *"Your position never gives you the right to command. It only imposes on you the duty of so living your life that others can receive your order without being humiliated."*

Although the disciples were slow to understand, they were the privileged ones. They had Jesus with them, ready to explain his teachings (Luke 8:10). The process of teaching them was long and arduous. Jesus did not relent. They had to pass from apprenticeship to discipleship, which they did, eventually. When they had gained some insights, he knew it was time to give them a task, *"And he sent them out to proclaim the Kingdom of God"* Luke 9: 2.

d) Springing to their defense: Since he had a relatively weak team, he had to constantly watch over them. Notice how he leaps to their defense when the Pharisees fault them: *"At that time Jesus went through the grain fields it, they said to him, 'Look, your disciples are doing what is not lawful to do on the Sabbath'. He said to them, 'Have you not read what David did when he and his companions were hungry? He entered the house of God and ate the bread of the Presence, which is not lawful for him or his companions to eat, but only for the priests'"* Matt 12:1-4. King David was among the more respected figures in the Old Testament. His example silenced the accusers. If he could eat the bread kept in the house of God, then the disciples of Jesus could eat grain plucked from the field. Besides, Scripture admonished farmers to grow grain on the fringes of fields to feed the hungry. So, the disciples were not breaking any law when they tried to satisfy their hunger.

Using Scripture (The Old Testament), the very weapon they used to inflict hurt on his disciples, he parried every thrust. With their weapon blunted, they saw no point in a sustained attack on his men; they retreated. This was just a war of words. Watch what he does when physical danger threatens his apostles. He throws himself between the soldiers and the disciples: *"So if you are looking for me, let these men go"* John 18:8. They knew that he was a problem-solver; they could count on him at all times.

e) Adopting different approaches: Knowing that each was different, he adopted different approaches, one might explain, different strokes for different folks. Let us look at some of those approaches. First, the disciples of John the Baptist, Andrew, and John, want to join Jesus but, they are timid and withdrawn. He does not wait for them to make the first move. He takes the initiative and speaks with them. Then they wish to know where he stays. He promptly invites them over and puts them at ease. Second, with Peter it is different. Peter has no inhibitions; open and ready. Jesus spots the potential in him and entrusts him with the responsibility of leading the rest. He wins warm praise but, a strong rebuke when he strays. Gaining maturity is a process. It takes time. It calls for patience and perseverance from the mentor. Peter was transformed through this maturing process, overseen by the Master. The firebrand Peter we see in the early chapters of the Gospels and the mellowed Peter we encounter in The Acts of the Apostles (a later part of the New Testament), confirms this transformation. Peter had matured and the master's touch was all too visible. Third, Philip followed Jesus when he was asked to follow but he needed clarification. Jesus spends time with him, keeping him enthralled in a long conversation. Fourth, Jesus praises Bartholomew (Nathaniel), and the one without guile loves it.

As seen in the four situations (and more in the Gospels), Jesus used different methods of tutoring his disciples to gain their trust. He got to the heart of his people and to the heart of the subject with a very simple and personal approach. Friendly, trusting and encouraging, he adapted to the needs of each, treating each in a special way. He was not distant or superior, rather he was close and accessible. How did he do it? By being with them constantly and demonstrating to them how his words could be translated into deeds. He interpreted his parables and teachings for them and united them into a cohesive team. Although most of the time, he had crowds around him, he concentrated on training his disciples. He would have to leave them behind, and they would have to be ready - each dealt with it differently.

f) Permitting freedom, not license: Such interactions with the Master gave them a sense of freedom. They could discuss his teachings with him freely as he listened to them intently. He clarified doubts, many times, if necessary (Mark 10:10). As someone rightly wrote, *"Doubt is one foot lifted, poised to step forward or backward. There is no motion until the foot comes down."* Doubts lead to questions, questions lead to answers, answers to acceptance, and then doubts are put to rest.

The foot comes down with a purpose. In a typical discussion, Peter puts it bluntly to the Lord, "What can we expect?" The answer Jesus gives him is not only complete but more importantly, unalloyed motivation. "Peter began to say to him, *'Look, we have left everything and followed you.'* Jesus said, *"Truly I tell you, there is no one who has left house or brothers or sisters or mother or father or children or fields, for my sake and for the sake of the good news who will not receive a hundredfold"* Mark 10: 28-30.

Such freedom of seeking clarification did not mean license. When they had to be chided, he did so without hesitation. Peter was questioned when he showed little faith (Matt 14:31) and the team was reprimanded (Mark 8:17) when their behavior baffled him. Very shrewdly he tested them (John 6:5-6) from time to time, cautioned them to be discreet (Luke 9:36), alert (Matt 24:50) and warned them against setting bad examples (Luke 17:1). Despite their closeness, there were times when he had to over-rule them.

This he did without flinching (Luke 18:15-16). Very rightly he maintained a healthy distance, not letting the relationship be taken for granted. There was respect, almost awe for the Master. With his disciples, he showed a fine balance had to be kept between freedom and discipline. One without the other would be counter-productive, as Cullen Hightower stressed: *"Discipline without freedom is tyranny. Freedom without discipline is chaos".*

g) Showing understanding: When a defaulting disciple repented, his sternness gave way to magnanimity and deep understanding. Peter denied Jesus, but later repented and wept bitterly. Not once did Jesus remind him of his denial. There was no reproach even in his tone. No change in his love for Peter. No demotion from the leadership position he had. On the contrary, Jesus confirmed Peter's appointment as the leader (John 21:16). Peter would be his successor.

Judas was not repentant but, Jesus shows no hostility, only understanding. When he brings soldiers to arrest him, he says: *"Friend, do what you are here to do"* Matt 26:50. As they await the traitor, Jesus asks his disciples to stay awake and pray with him. Instead, they fall asleep. Even at a critical hour, before his arrest, Jesus shows patience. He does not chastise them, there is only pain in his voice and sadness on his face.

h) Leading by example: Before beginning an intimate meal with his disciples, the Last Supper, Jesus gave them a lesson in humility. Normally, slaves performed the act of washing the feet of dinner guests. Here Jesus, the guest of honor, dressed like a slave, with a towel around his waist, insisted on washing the feet of his disciples. By doing so, he gave them a lasting example in humbly serving others. After he had washed their feet, he put on his robe and returned to the table. He said to them, *'Do you know what I have done to you? You call me Teacher and Lord - and you are right, for that is what I am. So if I, your Lord and Teacher, have washed your feet, you also ought to wash one another's feet; for I have set you an example that you also should do as I have done to you'"* John 13: 12-15.

He also set them powerful examples in decision-making, by being deliberate and purposeful. His decision to go to Jerusalem, where danger lurked, perplexed his disciples. His time for Calvary had come as he set his face in the direction of Jerusalem; dangers would not stop him. On threatening occasions in the past, he prudently chose to move out of harm's way, not this time. The disciples were in awe of his strong mind.

i) Identifying with them: He related so closely to the disciples that he identified himself with them, emphasizing, *"Whoever welcomes you, welcomes me"* Matt 10: 40. Luke puts the same thought in different words: *"Whoever listens to you listens to me, and whoever rejects you, rejects me"* Luke10:16. In response the disciples paid him a great tribute: *"And his disciples believed in him"* John 2: 11. The statement is rather simplistic but, it uncovers the pinnacle of faith they had climbed. When they learned Pharisees and Scribes proudly refused to accept Jesus, despite his great teachings, which were foretold in the Scriptures, the illiterate disciples rallied around him. He returned their compliment fittingly, *"You are those who stood by me in my trials"* Luke 22: 28.

j) Delegating: In time, and with training, the disciples were being groomed for higher responsibility. When the time for delegating was at hand, true delegation was given to them, with authority. Jesus did this, about two years into his public ministry. Sooner would have been catastrophic and later would have been too late. His timing was near perfect. He had selected simple folk like James and Andrew to represent him to the world. To them, he gave his own authority and power. First, he sent out the twelve, and later the seventy (Mark 6:7).

According to some, delegation, empowerment, is the willingness to let go and allow others to make mistakes. It is also the ability to establish and use broad controls for the team. Jesus followed these norms faithfully. His example would inspire his disciples to adopt similar measures. On their first assignment, he gave them broad guidelines. *"When they returned, they reported to him"* Mark 6:30. The joyful reporting symbolized a fulfillment of the task assigned to them. Even in those days, Jesus ensured they gained job satisfaction. Jesus also knew his team needed to take a break from their punishing schedule. The soul and body needed rest, which he gave them (Mark 6:31).

Jesus knew his life was short. His public ministry lasted a brief three years. His disciples had to be readied to carry on the task of fulfilling the Mission, teaching his message to the ends of the earth.
He had to move on, he could not tarry. The need to move on is explained with the right metaphor in the Biography of Vivekananda: *"How often does a man ruin his disciples by remaining always with them? When men are trained, it is essential that their leader leave them, for without his absence they cannot develop themselves. Plants always remain small under a big tree."* (Advaita Ashrama Mayavati).

k) Ensuring succession: We shall have to return to Peter. Despite his many weaknesses, Peter played a decisive role in managing the team. After the master's death, they were distraught and looked for some consolation in their old occupation, fishing. *"Simon Peter said to them, 'I am going fishing.' They said to him, 'we will go with you'"* John 21: 3. Note the difference, they do not say, 'we too will go fishing' but say, 'we will go with you'. This signified that they would follow him, their leader. Peter was given to expressing his loyalty to the Master.

He was rather boastful that he would not desert him, even if the others did forsake him. How wrong he was, became obvious, when he denied Jesus three times; only to repent and regain his position as head disciple. His brashness made him unafraid of friend or foe. He even chided the Master, *"And Peter took him aside and began to rebuke him (Jesus)"* Matt 16: 22. One cannot but appreciate the team culture, which the Master inculcated. Peter takes Jesus 'aside' to rebuke him, not in the presence of others.

We are tempted to put Peter down as the right-brain type, emotional, impulsive, brash, given to angry outbursts and rather predictable in his responses. His head was most often half a step behind his heart. Yet, his fire-in-the-belly attitude endeared him to both Master and the rest of the team. Could it have prompted his selection as a successor to Jesus? It is difficult to state with certainty. It is clear Jesus had confidence in him (Matt 16:18). With practical wisdom, Goethe wrote: *"Treat a man as he is and he will remain as he is; treat a man as he can and should be, and he will become as he can and should be."*

Would these words apply also to the way Jesus groomed Peter? Look at what became of Peter in the caring hands of the Master!

Only after Jesus died and rose from the dead, did they fully understand the true nature of the Kingdom he was setting in motion - it was primarily a spiritual kingdom and not a political power.
With the change in understanding came a dynamic transformation. His simple plan of action would be implemented using basic talents, skills, and strong faith in him. Compare the cowering disciples portrayed in the Gospels, with the bold and confident characters in the Acts of the Apostles. To the admiration of the common folk and the consternation of those in power, we see them perform works of extraordinary courage.

"It is the General who makes warriors of soldiers." Anon

* * *

Anjali leaned back in her chair and squatted one question in her mind: How do I compare with the standards Jesus set for his disciples? She found no answer. She had none.

Chapter Seven: The People Person

"The service we render to others is really the rent we pay for our room on this earth." W. Grenfell.

Oliva, the secretary to the CEO, had a problem with her computer. Instead of going through channels for getting the problem solved, she went directly to the top, to George. He heard her and requested his immediate junior to fix it for Oliva. The junior promptly handled his boss's request. On Thursday, Oliva was back in George's office. She thanked him for the immediate attention he gave her. She also inquired after his wife, Veronica, her classmate. Chatting for a while, she asked how he found the material Joseph gave him. Oliva had worked long hours on them, studying the papers in the process. When she heard that George enjoyed reading the sheets, she felt happy and asked how much he had left to read. He said he had read four of them and some of the Gospels. He added that he was planning to read the fifth article today.

* * *

People need to be reassured that a 'comfort-zone' operates if they are to draw near. They must feel wanted, free to interact, with no fear of a rebuff. That is why Jesus invited people to him with soothing and reassuring words, *"Come to me, all you that are weary and are carrying heavy burdens and I will give you rest"* Matt 11:28. John chooses different words to convey the same warmth: *"And anyone who comes to me I will never drive away"* John 6:37. People came - the poor and the needy, the sick and the challenged, the hungry and the weak, the depressed and the dejected, saints and sinners. Mixing freely with such people, he gave of his abundant generosity. He had come to serve his fellowmen. He would serve, without conditions. What stood out in these interactions was his empathy. His heart went out to those in trouble, finding ways to comfort them (Matt 9:36).

a) Dignified in giving: Although he was compassionate beyond measure, he was careful not to force himself on them. Like a true gentleman, he checked what they wanted of him: *"Then Jesus said to him, 'What do you want me to do for you?'"* Mark 10: 51. When they had made their requests, he satisfied their needs. We wonder why Jesus had to ask when the problem was apparent. Perhaps, Jesus wanted the crowd around him to know someone had a need, to which he was prepared to respond. By articulating his need, the recipient felt he was unloading a burden. The important inference is that, Jesus did not want to impose himself on anyone.

b) Humble and composed: His dignity in responding to the needs of his neighbors was born of his disarming humility. So real was his humility, people saw it and recognized it. Even in moments of triumph, he stayed composed (Mark 11:7-10), not exultant. As he entered Jerusalem, the crowds threw their clothing, cloaks and leafy branches on the road, while they shouted hosanna. There was no vainglory, only quiet acceptance of the triumphant moment. He knew the fickleness of the crowd. In a few days, those people would scream for his crucifixion and death.

c) Forgiving wrong doers: His ego was balanced and therefore he could view the failings of others with compassion, not accusation. The example he set from the cross has no parallel in history.

Physically abused and tortured by soldiers, reviled by crowds, and deserted by his friends, from the crucible of pain, he cries out, *"Father, forgive them; for they do not know what they are doing"* Luke 23:34. Some writers compare the death of Socrates to Jesus' death. Both lost their lives at the hands of their detractors. Socrates faced his end with a portion of Hemlock. Jesus suffered excruciating pain and death on the cross. Is a quiet death equal to a brutal and violent death? The comparison is odious. He preached forgiveness. Now, by example, he was living his teaching. His persecutors were being forgiven for their malice and hard-heartedness. He gave forgiveness a new dimension when he explained to Peter, *"Not seven times, but I tell you, seventy-seven times"* Matt 18:21-22.

In a parable, Jesus lays bare the consequences of not forgiving and not having mercy on others: *"For this reason, the Kingdom of heaven may be compared to a king who wished to settle accounts with his slaves. When he began the reckoning, one who owed him ten thousand talents was brought to him; and as he could not pay, his Lord ordered him to be sold, together with his wife and children and all his possessions, and payment to be made. So, the slave fell on his knees before him, saying, 'Have patience with me, and I will pay you everything'. And out of pity for him, the lord of that slave released him and forgave him the debt. But the same slave, as he went out came upon one of his fellow slaves who owed him a hundred denarii; and seizing him by the throat, he said, 'Pay what you owe'. Then his fellow slave fell down and pleaded with him, 'Have patience with me, and I will pay you'. But he refused; then he went and threw him into prison until he would pay the debt. When his fellow slaves saw what happened, they were greatly distressed, and they went and reported to their Lord all that had taken place. Then the Lord summoned him and said to him, 'You wicked slave! I forgave you all that debt because you pleaded with me. Should you not have had mercy on your fellow slave, as I had mercy on you?' And in anger, his lord handed him over to be tortured until he could pay his entire debt"* Matt 18:23-34.

Not forgiving those who offend us is not an option. Jesus makes it clear when he teaches his apostles to pray The Lord's Prayer. We can expect forgiveness from God only when we forgive others. Saint Paul gives a new twist to forgiveness. He says when you really want revenge – forgive. Why? Because when you forgive, you truly *'heap burning coals on their heads'* Romans 12: 20. They have to carry the burden of not really knowing why they were forgiven. The metaphor of burning coals is drawn from a Roman practice; someone who is forgiven carried on his head a pan of burning coals. A forgiven soul is in perpetual debt to the one who forgives him.

d) Self-effacing: His words and deeds had such an enormous impact on people. Even when he instructed them to keep his profile low, word of mouth praise could not be stopped. His fame spread far and wide, bringing to him wave upon wave of people. Some were so greatly influenced by him they wanted him to be their King. He would have none of it because he had not come to be their King in a political sense. He had come to show them a new way of life. John silences his critics who claim that he was self-seeking and bent on popularity: *"When Jesus realized that they were about to come and take him by force to make him King, he withdrew again to the mountain by himself"* John 6:15.

e) Fearless: To these qualities, he added fearlessness and openness. He feared no one. His idea of weathering the storm was to produce a stronger gale. Watch how he does it. *"At that very hour, some Pharisees came and said to him, 'Get away from here, for Herod wants to kill you.' He said to them, 'Go and tell that fox from me---'"* Luke 13: 31-32. Tale carriers would ensure the comment reached the ears of Herod, the king. Yet, Jesus did not fear him. Even against the Scribes who were a powerful sect, whose favors one tried to win, he was plain and decisive in his rebuttal (Luke 20:45-46).

Jesus had no need for such double-dealing power brokers. So strong was his courage of conviction, even his adversaries grudgingly praised it: *"And you show deference to no one, but teach the way of God in accordance with the truth"* Luke 20: 21. In support of his openness and honesty, he said: *"I have spoken openly to the world; I have always taught in the synagogues and in the temple, where all the Jews come together. I have said nothing in secret"* John 18: 20.

f) Not wanting sympathy: He drew strength from within himself, so he needed little or no emotional support from others. Even in his darkest hour, when everyone had forsaken him, Jesus did not look for pity or sympathy. Addressing weeping women who lined the path to Calvary he deflected attention they gave him, to get them to understand what lay in store for them: *"Daughters of Jerusalem, do not weep for me, but weep for yourselves and for your children"* Luke 23: 28. He did not want their tears.

g) Expecting faith: All he asked for was trust in his words and works. Many times, during his public ministry he asked those who came to him if they had faith in him. On one occasion here is how he checked: *"Do you believe that I am able to do this?* They said to him, *'Yes Lord'"* Matt 9: 28.

h) Seizing the initiative: As a people-person, he believed he should seize the initiative and not wait for the other person to step forward. In the meeting with Zacchaeus, he demonstrated how he took such initiatives (Luke 19:5). Zacchaeus, short in stature, had climbed a tree to get a glimpse of Jesus. Now, he was an important man, the chief tax collector but, he was also an unscrupulous defrauder. He retained money for himself from the tax he collected. Acting as a change agent, Jesus takes the initiative to talk to him. He did not avoid him because he was corrupt or wait for him to start the conversation. We also recall the selection of his apostles when Jesus took the initiative, each time, to choose them.

i) Using the power of praise: How does Jesus fare in interpersonal skills? Jesus knew the power of praise and used it effectively. He readily gave praise and extolled virtue. To the Centurion who showed enormous faith, he gave warm praise, *"When he entered Capernaum, a centurion came to him, appealing to him and saying, 'Lord, my servant is lying at home paralyzed, in terrible distress.' And he said to him, 'I will come and cure him.' The centurion answered, 'Lord, I am not worthy to have you come under my roof; but only speak the word and my servant will be healed. For I also am a man under authority, with soldiers under me; and I say to one, "go', and he goes, and to another, "come', and he comes, and to my slave, "Do this', and the slave does it'. When Jesus heard him, he was amazed and said to those who followed him, 'Truly I tell you, in no one in Israel have I found such faith'"* Matt 8: 5-10.

John the Baptist, Jesus' cousin and a prophet in his own right, showed great courage in challenging the evil ways of King Herod. Openly opposing the king, at that time, had serious consequences like imprisonment, and death. But John the Baptist was fearless and Jesus compliments him (Matt 11:11). And he extols the faith of the Canaanite woman who showed exemplary confidence when she pleaded her daughter's case with him (Matt 15:28). Even little acts of little people were recognized and praised. The poor widow could put into the temple treasury only two copper coins, which is less than a penny. Jesus praises her (Mark 12:43-44). But praise was held back when he read the minds of people and found in them evil thoughts (Matt 9:4). So, with Jesus, there were no favorites. Good deeds were praised, and the brazen deeds of seemingly important people were bared, for them to realize their misdeeds, repent and make amends.

He warned against over-confidence and complacency. Do not take your place for granted, he cautioned: *"But many who are first will be last, and the last will be first"* Mark 10: 31. Do-gooders among the Pharisees believed their law-abiding, righteous behavior gave them the right to God's friendship. Jesus lost no time in warning them that their over-confidence would be their nemesis. God's love was a gift, he asserted. Combining the power of praise with the potency of rewards, he evolved a winning formula, which was the motivation at its best: *"Truly I tell you none of these will lose their reward"* Matt 10: 42. He promised such rewards even to his disciples. They needed such motivation because they left everything behind to follow him.

j) Resolving conflicts: Where there are people, there are conflicts and conflicts lead to hatred and hostility. What did Jesus have to say? Never let differences snowball. Resolve them at once, *"So when you are offering your gift at the altar, if you remember that your brother or sister has something against you, leave your gift there before the altar and go; first, be reconciled to your brother or sister, and then come and offer your gift"* Matt 5: 23-24. Mark his words: 'If your brother or sister has something against you' and not, 'if you have something against your brother or sister', which meant even if you did not have hostile feelings against the other, go and be reconciled. Be pro-active in resolving conflicts and forgiving. We cannot help admiring his commonsense approach to resolving conflicts, face-to-face: *"If another member of the church sins against you, go and point out the fault when the two of you are alone* (Protect his dignity). *If the member listens to you, you have regained that one. But if you are not listened to, take one or two others along with you, so that every word may be confirmed by the evidence of two or three witnesses"* Matt 8: 15.

What we have seen here are the multi-faceted skills of Jesus in transacting with people, as the people-person. He was always eager to help the poor and needy. To the hungry and weak, he gave speedy relief. The depressed and dejected returned with hope and confidence. The saints were confirmed in their holiness and sinners were reconciled with God. He did not drive away anyone who went to him, instead, he gave them rest and lightened their burden. Whatever their distress, Jesus asked them to shun worry (Matt 6:34), because he was there to address their concerns, if only they had faith in him. He could do this for others because he himself had walked through fire. Don't we use the expression: *'he has been through the mill'*? It is a tribute we pay such a person. What we really mean is that through the trials he faced and the sufferings he endured, he has been strengthened and ennobled; and now is a better human being. Now, he can reach out, understand, and empathize. He can now be trusted, for trust is the ultimate tribute you can pay him. They could trust Jesus, and he would honor their trust.

* * *

George stared at the papers in front of him. He was troubled. What if he were to die today? How many people would really miss him? Did he relate to people like Jesus did? What was holding him back? Despite his rank and status, was his life satisfying?

Chapter Eight: Perceptions of the Model

"Know then this truth, enough for man to know, virtue alone is happiness below." A. Pope.

On Thursday evening, to be at home as Suman returned from her day at school, Sammy left the factory a little early. After snacks and tea, Sammy moved a chair to the balcony, and resumed the reading of papers Joseph gave him. He asked Suman if she had read the article on the history of Jesus' time. She had, and added she made some notes from the article. She was going to use them in a class on ancient history for some of her senior students. Sammy was glad that she also found merit in the article. Would she enjoy the other papers in the bundle, he asked himself? Why not? He planned to share with her all the sheets so they could discuss them. With a tall glass of cold beer by his side, he began reading.

* * *

Though he walked among ordinary men, Jesus was no ordinary man. He walked tall. It explains why he evoked different and strong reactions among people who did not walk tall. Many openly admired him, a few felt threatened by him, and many did not conceal their hostility. People's reactions plunged from heady exhilaration to murderous rejection. His last days on earth included one scene of triumph, as people roared their approval when he made a grand entry into Jerusalem. Even with a tumultuous welcome, Jesus sat, painfully aware their praise was hollow and passing. Despite such opposed responses, he held out his hand in friendship. *'Have no fear, Peace be with you, Have faith'*, he would only speak kind words. No condescension, only compassion.

The Gospels paint a picture of Jesus in different colors – perceptions of different people.

1) Let us look at the brush strokes of **people in high places**: Pilate, the Roman Governor in Palestine, The Roman Centurion, and Jarius, a leader from the Synagogue. *"Then Pilate said to the chief priests and the crowds, 'I find no basis for an accusation against this man.'"* Luke 23: 4. The Roman Centurion who led the soldiers in their Governor-given-assignment to crucify Jesus could not hold back his praise: *"When the centurion saw what had taken place* (at the crucifixion), *he praised God and said 'certainly this man was innocent'"* Luke 23: 47. Stiff-necked leaders of the Synagogue did not bend low before Jesus. Jairus was an exception: *"Then one of the leaders of the synagogue named Jairus came and, when he saw him* (Jesus), *fell at his feet and begged him repeatedly" Mark 5:22.*

2) Besides people in high places, Nicodemus and Joseph of Arimathea, disciples of Jesus in secret, were also **important persons and contemporaries.** After Jesus died, these men sought permission from Pilate to claim the body of Jesus for burial. They bought a hundred pounds of myrrh and aloes to treat the bruised and battered body of their master before burial. A few pounds would have been enough. But they would follow the dictates of their hearts. It would be a hundred pounds. The cost did not count; for here was no ordinary man who was dead. John the Baptist, a prophet respected by many, was a contemporary. What colors did John the Baptist add to the picture? He proclaimed, *"The one who is more powerful than I is coming after me, I am not worthy to stoop down and untie the thongs of his sandals"* Mark 1:7.

3) What were the perceptions of his **disciples**? Two of them traveling to Emmaus had Jesus (incognito) walk with them. In ecstasy, they exclaimed their hearts were alight when he was speaking with them (Luke 24:32). We have already seen how his twelve disciples regarded him.

4) And what did his **customers** (crowds, who packed fields and riverbanks and seashores to listen to him, and watch him perform wondrous deeds), have to say? What mix of colors did they use? *"Jesus departed with his disciples to the sea, and a great multitude from Galilee followed him; hearing all that he was doing, they came to him in great numbers from Judea, Jerusalem, Idumaea, beyond the Jordan, and the region around Tyre and Sidon"* Mark 3:7-8. In chapters 4 and 5 of his Gospel, Luke's words border the superlative to convey what they think of him, *"All spoke well of him and were amazed at the gracious words that came from his mouth"* Luke 4:22.

"Amazement seized all of them, and they glorified God and were filled with awe, saying, 'We have seen great things today'" Luke 5:26. So strong was public opinion in his favor, that those who connived to put him to death were fearful of the crowd backlash. They waited for a chance to take him when he was alone: *"So, he* (Judas) *consented and began to look for an opportunity to betray him to them* (Pharisees and High Priests) *when no crowd was present"* Luke 22:6. Often, crowds are silk on one side and sandpaper on the other. Manipulated by vested interests, they turned unfriendly now and again (John 7:12). One can

connect the swing in their emotions with the way Jesus polarized opinions. He boldly contrasted his teachings with the words and actions of his opponents.

To assail him with questions and verbal traps, spies were planted among onlookers. Jesus knew he was not safe anywhere, but he could not avoid the crowds because they sought him everywhere. The hostility of the crowds wore off quickly and they were back listening, applauding, being fed and healed, and following him in large numbers. Many times, they tried to make him king, but he would not accept glory on any terms. In truth, he sought no glory at all. Despite his attempts to stifle the publicity his actions merited, the powerbrokers felt threatened and huddled, scheming and plotting (Mark 11:11) Their apparent triumph at the crucifixion looked jaded as the criminal, hanging from a cross next to Jesus, proclaimed Jesus was guiltless (Luke 23:41).Together, those in high places, his contemporaries, disciples, and customers proclaim his goodness. The verdict from them is the same, he spoke good words and performed great deeds.

How did Jesus react to them? How did he see himself? When the disciples of John the Baptist asked who he was, he gave them an account of his personal effectiveness. His credentials were beyond question, *"And he answered them, 'Go and tell John what you have seen and heard'"* Luke 7: 22. There was nothing to hide. In explaining his role, he likens himself to a shepherd, a metaphor easily understood by the crowd, *"I am the Good Shepherd. The Good Shepherd lays down his life for his sheep"* John 10:11.

The connection with his Mission Statement is too obvious to escape attention. As part of his mission, he had come to serve his fellow man. To make it possible, he made himself accessible to the common people. People were happy to meet him and invite him over to visit. He went graciously and returned their hospitality when he had them over (especially the poor), to share his meager rations, consistent with the recommendation he made, *"When you give a banquet, invite the poor, the crippled, the lame, and the blind. And you will be blessed because they cannot repay you"* Luke 14:13-14.

How often have we known of ideas that would not blossom, of products that would not be made, of careers that would not take off, and companies that would not join the Big League, because of a crippling malady, we call *'fear of failure'*? Jesus did not suffer from this paralyzing affliction. He performed because of his strong beliefs. He performed despite his detractors. He performed because of his overflowing compassion. He loved deeply, and his love was expressed in different ways.

What any leader would love to hear, what any professional would want on his appraisal form, came to Jesus unsolicited, from his customers. *"They were astounded beyond measure, saying, 'He has done everything well'"* Mark 7:37

* * *

Sammy rose through the ranks as an upright professional - not compromising on ethics, not trying to humor the hierarchy, and not slackening his pace, even when times were good. Now he had doubts. Had he done enough? Were members of his team inspired by him, or were they responding to his rank? What were the perceptions of people? Did he have to check, or rely on feedback he got occasionally? He was confused. So, he decided to check with Joseph at their next appraisal meeting.

Chapter Nine: Some Lessons for Professionals

"We are all angels with one wing; we can fly while embracing each other." Luciano de Crescenzo.

It was late on Thursday evening when George and Veronica were listening to Beethoven's violin concerto. The strains from the cadenza wafted into the adjoining rooms. Intoxicated with their favorite piece, they were in a stupor for a time, until George roused himself into action – he had much to cover of the papers he took from Joseph. Quickly, he grabbed the papers and asked Veronica to join him. They would both read, she first and he next. In an enthusiastic voice, she began to read.

* * *

In chapters 5, 6, 7 and 8, we watched Jesus perform. We marveled at the many sides of his towering personality and were edified by the wonders he performed in relating to people and situations. Now, it is time to draw inferences. Can we learn from him? Can he be a model? Let us begin with his mission.

How does Jesus connect with the business world?

a) The message of love is universal; it is for all – professionals are not excluded. The first part of the message is to love God. Loving God is the choice each makes. Many are happy loving him. Some try to deny him. Some others are indifferent. They think they can exclude God from their lives. Although they want to wriggle out of God's embrace, his arms encircle all; he makes no exceptions. The choice is theirs to accept him or not, but loving others, which is the second part, is not optional. Why? The psychiatrist Alfred Adler has the answer, *"All human failures are the result of a lack of love."* When we refuse to love and help others, why would they love and help us? It is stating the obvious, we need others in the network of life, even as others need us. We are de-bonded when we do not hold helping hands and when we refuse to clasp imploring hands. We need our families, our employers, our peers, our customers, and many others. No one is outside the loop, and we are in the loop that others construct. The brotherhood of man, like the Fatherhood of God, is as vital as the air we breathe. The third part of the message on love is the love of self. Thankfully, we need no coaxing to love ourselves.

b) We may love others without having to serve them. But we **cannot genuinely serve others without loving them.** We cannot serve our families and our professional associates without respecting their interests. When (b) – serving others – is in place, then (a) - loving others – has gone ahead. The two – (a) and (b) - work together. When we treat every relationship as a customer-relationship, in our interest, and of the corporation, we build goodwill, culminating in customer-delight, and profit from such transactions.

c) **Getting wrongdoers to repent** and mend their ways may appear to be outside our professional purview. But in truth, it is not. How do we explain it? Why do we have appraisals in the professional context, if not to suggest improvement; if not to correct those who err? Why should we worry over the failing performances of our colleagues? Why should we take credit for the positive performance of teammates, when we counsel them? Why do we try to repeatedly correct those who are in our team?

It is because we fall when they fall. To stop them from falling we must use our strength and capabilities. No, we professionals cannot turn away from wrong-doers or poor performers.

What is the message for professionals drawn from Jesus' beliefs? In corporate circles, Jesus' teachings and his beliefs may seem idealistic, rather impracticable. He silences his detractors with a parable of huge, pragmatic dimensions. *"He put before them another parable: The kingdom of heaven may be compared to someone who sowed good seeds in his field; but while everybody was asleep, an enemy came and sowed weeds among the wheat. When the plants came up and bore grain, the weeds also appeared. The slaves of the householder came and said to him, 'Master, didn't you sow good seed in your field? Where did these weeds come from?' He answered, 'An enemy has done this.' The slaves responded, 'Do you want us to go and gather them?' He replied, 'No; for in gathering the weeds you would uproot the wheat along with them. Let both of them grow together until the harvest; and at harvest time I will tell the reapers, collect the weeds first and bind them in bundles to be burned, but gather the wheat into my barn'"* Matt 13:24-30. We cannot but admire his discerning response. Wait. **There are times we shall have to suffer some evil in the larger interests of operations,** but not for long. A predetermined compromise will have to be made for long term gains. Not in principles. Not in basics. There will be no compromise on the truth or on integrity. Jesus does not forget the practical side.

The Gospels recount many more beliefs Jesus shared with his listeners. We have listed a few here, that focus significantly on professionals.

a) The Golden Rule: *"In everything, do to others as you would have them do to you"* Matt. 7:12. Professionals pursue interests at the cost of others. They must win. Losing is not an option. To win they will adopt any means. Winning makes them smug. They climb the victory stand to applause that is deafening. One wonders, are they happy? If they face themselves, as they should, they may find dark recesses needing light. Some parts of them are alien to the whole. That is why the Golden Rule makes sense.

We cannot find joy in walking over others. We cannot live in peace with pyrrhic victories. We must value others as we value ourselves and adopt a win-win attitude, to avoid failure that is inevitable when love is missing – in the words of Alfred Adler. If we don't like to be walked over, how does it make sense to walk over others? When we treat others badly, we give them a reason to retaliate. The Golden Rule is not just for the weak who cannot fight back. It is for the strong and powerful. It is for all, professionals and non-professionals.

b) One cannot serve two masters. One cannot serve God and Satan at the same time. One cannot compromise on ethics and believe operations are clean. One cannot be deceitful and put on a straight face. One cannot ignore fair play and expect fairness from others. Duplicity will exact a price sooner than later. And, professional choices have to be right, in the short and long term.

c) To be wise: Many professionals pride themselves in being clever, smart, on top of all they do. It is a nice feeling, but an empty feeling. Unless they are wise (and we all know what that means) their deeds will haunt them, because short term gains do not live long term. Expediency is fraught with risks. And down the road, there is always someone smarter. Honesty and Fidelity are expressions of wisdom: In an Indian vernacular, a saying is: *'The one who cheats repeatedly will be caught soon'*. History has shown it to be true. Disclosures of wrongdoing in the professional world no more surprise us – they happen every day. We have lost our sense of sin; lost our moral compass. Our conscience is appeased with the argument 'everyone is doing it,' it is okay. Distressingly, our children use the same logic. We then perpetuate wrongdoing. And fidelity to the corporation is not negotiable. Grouses over pay and perks, unhappiness on how we are treated, dissatisfaction with unfair company policies and fatigue over long hours do not justify unfaithfulness or betrayal. If the burden is too heavy, shed it; move to a place where expectations are met but do not stay dissatisfied and betray the company. It is a test of character, to be honest, and true.

d) Attitude to wealth: The temptation to make unlawful gains is irresistible; the logic compelling – many others are doing it and apparently happy. We stain our hands and cannot wash them clean. Why does this happen? The inordinate attachment we have toward profits, possessions, and pleasure drives us into acts we would not normally perform. Sane men go insane under the influence of such enticements, and professionals are no exception.

e) Attitude to enemies: The pity is that competition is regarded as an enemy to be crushed under-foot. To achieve that end we employ fair or foul means; more often than not the means are unwarranted. To silence the competitor within the organization, we scheme and plot his/her downfall. Are we in peace after that? Should we not reckon with the enemy, who is plotting our downfall; who is pulling out long knives? Where will this senseless battle end? Would it not be better to adopt the abundance mentality 'of live and let live'? Would it not be better to be gracious and absolve others who wrong us? Leave them to worry about why we forgave them as we heap burning coals on their heads.

f) Truth: Is the choice of being truthful open to debate? Is the path of truth shrouded by doubt when millions of dollars are involved? When a coveted position is at stake? When personal loss is imminent? If it is a question of personal priority and convenience, what lessons shall we teach those who hope to learn from us - our children; our juniors? Only the truth will set us and our children free – Jesus was specific.

g) Respect: *"Employees who feel respected are more satisfied with jobs and more grateful and loyal to their companies."* That is the point Kristie Rogers is trying to make in an article, *'Do your employees feel respected?'* in The Harvard Business Review of July-August 2018. Respect is a time-saver, not a time-waster – is a strong point that emerges from the article. Owned respect is the first phase when the company respects the employee for who s/he is. Earned respect is the next phase, when the employee merits praise and recognition, through good performance. And, because of both - owned and earned respect - a ripple effect is set in motion when employees begin to respect their customers. Notice what happened with Jesus and his team. Their backgrounds were inappropriate – to state the least. Yet, Jesus did not make them feel inadequate. Teaching them, guiding them and being with them for most of the time, he helped them take baby steps in the direction of his mission. They were slow to learn, yet he was patient with them, explaining the same point many times until they understood. He readily forgave their lapses and encouraged them as they performed small acts. Recall their return from the first trip they made on their own.

Jesus listened to them intently and commended the good work they did. Slowly they gained confidence in themselves and basked in the warmth of respect they got from Jesus. Who profited? Their customers, the people who surrounded them. Their numbers grew. They were comfortable in the presence of Jesus and his disciples, and they listened.

George signaled to Veronica to stop reading. He took over.

h) Is Jesus' knowledge a yardstick for professionals? Can professionals be inspired by the knowledge Jesus had? They can, when they decide to gain knowledge of their functions, products, markets, competition, and people. The knowledge they have, when translated into strategies and implemented faithfully will bring desired results. Jesus showed how his knowledge amazed others. Professionals can use their great knowledge to astound themselves and the competition. Knowledge is always a strength, as it was for Jesus.

i) What can professionals learn from the work habits of Jesus? Management thinkers of old and of the present insist on the same basics. You go to the customer and don't wait for him to come to you. Plan operations in detail, work the plan and always take your people with you. The work habits that Jesus had were the same, though he operated 2000 years ago. It only showed that he was far ahead of his time. In fact, he set the stage for professionals of all time – they have something to learn from him. Many professionals try to work hard; plan their work and work their plan. But the question remains: What are their motives? Their interests are to be safeguarded – there is no doubt. But do the interests of others figure in their calculations? Does their own Corporation rank high on their list of priorities? Will their hard work benefit others, even as it rewards them? Jesus answered all these questions in his faultless life when he showed that others mattered; his motives were beyond question.

j) What can professionals learn from his team management skills? Roger Dow and Susan Cook make some interesting points in their book, *"Turned On"* (Harper Business). They insist that the Team leader should keep the team focused on the big picture. He should get them pulling on the same side by connecting one to the other. And, communicate with them to get them involved in goal accomplishment. The authors go on to make the point: A leader should be a good human being. Winston Churchill, Martin Luther King Jr., and Mother Teresa had very different styles, but each could get people to rally round a cause. The leader's integrity and strength of character secure the trust and dedication of his or her people. That is why the words of Ann Landers make sense: *"Character is what you are willing to do when the spotlight has been turned off, the applause has died down and no one is around to give you credit."* Character is that intangible that is tangible in the leader. The Gospels recount occasions when Jesus was acclaimed, but he shied away from recognition. He shunned the spotlight. He was the same in and out of the spotlight.

Commenting on the facets of leadership, Dow and Cook state that leaders come in different shapes and sizes. The title does not make a leader, but his attributes and commitment complete the portrait. Leaders see themselves as resource persons, teaching, inspiring, and motivating the team. Essentially, by setting the right example and by caring deeply about the team, he or she sets the tempo.
The picture they paint of a leader has shades mixed so well, one can only behold the finished work with admiration. Now look at the shades they pick: *"I think you must be a little bit strict, a little bit strong, a lit bit friendly and a little bit encouraging."* A little bit of each shade to paint the perfect picture.

How does Jesus match the picture of a leader that the authors paint? With Jesus, his Mission was paramount. His chosen disciples were persuaded to understand and accept the Mission. He gave them specific instructions, so they knew what to do even in tough times. On the one hand, he empowered them; on the other, he held them accountable. In time, his Mission became their Guiding Principle. Many of the disciples died as martyrs for the cause. Many read that as an anti-climax. Is martyrdom success? In their lexicon, it was because they did not measure their success by wealth and fame, but by standards that Jesus set for them, which was to live a life of love and die loving even those who put them to death. Strange, but lofty!

Jesus ensured that the disciples mixed freely. He made small teams handle special assignments. He reminded them of their unique role; that they were chosen for a great purpose. He instilled confidence in them and built on their strengths, gently correcting them. He identified with them. He was with them for most of the three years of his public ministry, leading by example; teaching, clarifying, demonstrating to them. He did not ignore even matters of little importance. He delegated responsibility with authority; and molded the team into a cohesive whole. The four Gospels have many passages to show his deep caring and constant concern. He reached out to his team, consoling, encouraging, educating and helping them. He listened, empathized and readily forgave. He cared even when it hurt him most. In essentials, he fostered unity; in non-essentials, he gave them liberty and in everything he embraced them in love. From him, they learned that *'life is love's brief tournament' Anon.*

In chapter 6 we read of the different facets of his team management. In choosing his team, his charisma came into play. It is important for recruiters to remember that. The profile of the company helps, but the charisma of the interviewer casts a spell on the candidate. Jesus chose to keep the team structure lean, simple and effective. Professionals need to guard against many levels in a structure. Too many levels create a distance, too few take away a healthy distance. To find the right structure is a test of professional maturity. Jesus managed his weak team through a combination of different but effective methods; Situational Management was one. Today's professionals are urged to follow in his footsteps because managing a weak team is more taxing and challenging than getting results out of a gifted team.

Abraham Lincoln, one of the great leaders of all time, transformed not just himself, but also his divided team, manifesting his sterling qualities, one of which was his sure-footed confidence. In her article, in the Harvard Business Review of September-October 2018, titled: Lincoln and the Art of Transformative Leadership, Doris Kearns Goodwin, makes a strong case for one of the four kinds of leadership: **1) Transformative, 2) Crisis management 3) Turnaround and 4) Visionary.** To establish her premise, she lists the qualities of Lincoln, a transformative leader, who led the country through the controversial period of the Civil War and freedom for slaves. He began with a divided team but ended the Proclamation of freedom with a team that solidly backed him. Now that his roots were deep, he had no reason to fear the storm.

What were the transformative qualities of Lincoln? He could spot contending viewpoints, know when to hold back and when to move forward, set an example, understand the emotional needs of his team, refuse to let past resentment fester, control angry impulses, protect colleagues from blame, win over skeptics, keep his word, gauge sentiment and earn trust.

Was Jesus a transformative leader? In him did the strands come together. Let us examine facts against the checklist the Doris Kearns Goodwin provides. Since Jesus lived more than 1800 years before Lincoln, he could not have copied the American; instead, there is a fair chance that the converse was true because Jesus was authentic and exercised authority even without a title.

Without making it obvious, Jesus not only anticipated but also harmonized opposing views. Judas, who was known to have contacts with the Sanhedrin, preferred a high-profile projection of Jesus. Simon the leper, who had swallowed the bitter pill of disfigurement – and was cured by Jesus – advised a low-profile start with a slow and prudent build-up. Jesus reconciled their views when he became the champion of the poor, not the upper classes, who the religious elders favored.

Jesus knew when to advance and when to retreat. For most of his ministry, he covered both friendly and unfriendly territories. Instigated by the elders, when the people turned against him and became hostile, Jesus retreated, for a short time, to a relatively safe area – Ephraim – and continued his work there. No bravado, only wise withdrawal. Like new shoots that stick out to check if the day is right to grow, his disciples scanned the scene to determine when Jesus could return to his routine.

Setting an example came to him naturally. When he washed the feet of the disciples – a task relegated to slaves – Jesus set them an example in humility that was difficult to match. His overarching purpose was to love and serve God and fellowmen. His words and deeds were so strong that his disciples would rather die than abandon his teachings.

He not only understood the physical stress of his disciples who followed him, and asked them to come apart and rest awhile, but also resonated with their troubled emotional needs – the disquieting truth did not unsettle him. He understood Peter's fear of torture, which drove him to denial of his Mater, and the power-lust of James and John, who wished to share power with their Lord. He responded fittingly and compassionately, in each case.

Never to nurse grudges, Jesus was always ready to forgive offenders. From the cross, he forgave all his persecutors because he would not let negative thoughts get the better of him. Like a searing iron, he cauterized anything that was against God's will.

Although he was provoked by the opposition, time and again, he stayed calm and gave them reason-based answers, not emotion-charged rebuttals. Like the two wings of a bird that lifts it to heights, his sense of fair play and justice made him soar over trifling issues. He would not swoop to prevail!

When the Pharisees accused his disciples of stealing grain on the Sabbath, Jesus defended his men by quoting King David – the Jewish icon. Their accusers were silenced. At his capture by Judas and his band,

Jesus threw himself against the ruffians, demanding that his disciples be spared. He was unchanging and unchangeable!

Thomas was a skeptic, doubting the resurrection of Jesus. Jesus then appeared to his disciples and showed him his wounds and obliterated all his doubts. Thomas prostrated in faithful surrender.

Whether he made travel plans or scheduled teaching sessions, Jesus always kept his promise. He was master of his words, not a slave of his mouth. Perhaps, his resurrection on the third day, as promised, was the highpoint of his remarkable life of truth and faithfulness.

He gauged the sentiment of his listeners and opened his teaching with a suitable parable. And, on more than one occasion he fed them when he sensed they were hungry and tired. The trust people expressed in him before they were healed was a reflection of the growing confidence they had in his powers and goodness. For them, meeting him was like visiting a shrine – holiness radiated from him. The disciples left everything and followed him, in an expression of implicit faith. In their simplicity, they chose to give God (they believed he was the Messiah) the best of their time, not what was left.

Jesus excelled not only in transformative leadership but, also in the other three:
1) Time after time, he found himself confronting a hostile opposition. He would not run away, instead, he faced them with composure and demolished their arguments. No rancor at all! In the crisis of betrayal by Judas, he showed manliness and courage of an unusual level. Even his adversaries admired him in secret.
2) He was a turnaround specialist. Consider his visit to Samaria – an unfriendly territory. When he left, after just a few days, he had become their hero. They followed and obeyed him.
3) Was he a visionary? There is no doubt he was a visionary. Go over the verses in the Bible which extoll his approach for the future. Stake the present for the future, the eternal future, was his dictum. What you hoard on earth perishes, not what you gather for eternal life. He cautioned them to take it in stages. Make it possible, then easy, until it becomes effortless.

In short, Jesus was a complete leader, combining four kinds of leadership. Some of the methods Jesus adopted:

a) Getting his team to commit to his mission, in quiet hope, not bitter resignation.

b) He gained their obedience, they lived in a state of perpetual excitement.
c) To give them confidence in him, he continually sprang to their defense. They felt secure in his leadership.
d) To make them feel wanted, he treated them differently, without acting superior.
e) Giving them friendship, he struck a balance between freedom and discipline.
f) Leading by example, he understood each and responded to their needs.
g) He planned for succession, so there was be no vacuum in leadership.

The lesson on leadership, as recorded in the Gospels, is an incredible teaching tool.

* * *

As George finished reading, he asked himself a rhetorical question, "When can we, at Mount Pharmaceuticals, aspire to reach such daunting heights?"
Veronica was pensive but added: "As long as there is hope, the effort is worthwhile."

Chapter Ten: Jesus Appraised

"Assuredly nobody will care for him who cares for nobody."
Thomas Jefferson.

Bangalore, India, is about 200 miles from Chennai (earlier known as Madras). It is a short journey by train. Lissy was planning to make the trip and was packing a few belongings and gifts, for her visit of two days. Lissy's brother, Tony, had bought a new apartment in Bangalore. He invited her family to join him in the celebrations. However, Lambert could not attend. He was meeting with an important customer on Saturday. Lissy and son Augustus would leave on Friday evening and return on Monday morning. Lambert was reconciled to the idea of spending the weekend alone. His plans were to catch up on some reading and sending some personal emails. His plans changed on Friday morning.

On Friday morning, Joseph checked in but left early, since he wasn't feeling well. He called Lambert and explained that the meeting scheduled for Friday afternoon would have to be rescheduled.
"We'll have to fix another time." Joseph was apologetic.
"No problem," Lambert reassured him, "How does Sunday suit you?"
"Fine by me, please, check with the others."
"Lissy is out of town and I am alone. Perhaps we could meet at my place. We'll be left to ourselves."
"That is great!"
"I'll have Olivia call you after we have checked with the others," Lambert suggested.
"Okay, thanks." Joseph hung up.
They were to meet at Lambert's house on Sunday morning. There was to be no order or sequence in the discussion; they were going to freewheel. To keep things going, Ravi would stand by to fetch food, coffee, sandwiches, and other odds and ends.
At 11:05 on Sunday, the meeting started with Joseph apologizing for the postponement. He hinted that the rescheduling may have given them, providentially, more time to read the New Testament and the other reading material. He requested Richard to make notes.
"Out of some evil, much good comes," he philosophized.
"Yes, I read through Mathew, Mark and the other sheets," Richard announced.
"I also had time to read them," Anjali added.
"I am one step ahead, I read Mathew, Mark, and Luke, plus the other papers," Sammy responded.

"I have read the Gospels many times. My mother made sure of it. But I have not reflected on them like Joseph," Lambert was being modest.

Only George had not spoken. All eyes turned to him.

With customary caution, he began, "You see, when we spoke on Wednesday, I was rather abrupt and unprofessional. Joseph's note struck a chord in me. I argued with myself. After all, we were not getting into a religious discourse. We were only looking at professional stuff. Could we find something in Jesus? If he had something to offer, what was wrong with looking at his wisdom? I convinced myself I was wrong, and I owe you an apology for my terse reactions., Now, to give you proof of my goodwill, like Joseph and Lambert, I read all four of the Gospels, and the extra sheets," he said with some satisfaction.

Joseph put his hands together and started a slow clap. The others joined in. George colored, putting up his hands he said, "Thank you, you are kind."

"We are starting well, why not George lead the discussion?" Joseph suggested.

George protested and so did other VP's, all thought Joseph should lead.

"Okay, the team decision will be honored." Joseph gave in.

"How shall we put points together?" he asked, ensuring the lead went back to his team.

"Perhaps by attempting a 360-degree appraisal of Jesus," Richard proposed.

"Absolutely brilliant, there's no better way to do it," said Joseph, bullish on the idea.

"That's a great idea," Anjali echoed.

"So, why don't you start, Richard?" Joseph urged.

"A word of caution, since we do not know how the 360-degree appraisal is administered in India, we have to be careful in stating our opinions. In applying the system, we are not even novices. Let's go about it cautiously. It may seem okay, looking at a person in history but, we have to be fair in our assessment." Richard mentioned solemnly.

"Stated like a true HR man," Lambert complimented.

"The 90-degree appraisal is not possible. Jesus reported to no one. For feedback from peers, teammates, and customers, we have plenty of evidence in the Gospels," Richard stated, looking for support; everyone nodded in agreement.

Joseph stepped in, "Unless we place Pilate, the Roman Governor, in the role of a superior."

Lambert spoke up, "Even if we do, Pilate found no fault in Jesus. He was visibly impressed with his behavior and tried hard to set him free. Pilate was a coward, he succumbed to public pressure."

George shared an insight: "You are right, Lambert. What struck me is the role of Roman Governor, Pilate. He was a very senior professional in the Roman hierarchy. Yet, he is not the one who inspires me. Pilate, the professional, is dwarfed in the presence of the super-professional, Jesus, whom he crucified."

"Very profound observation, George," Joseph stated admiringly.

"So, the first quadrant in the 360-degree appraisal gets favorable remarks. Okay by all?" Richard was looking for a quick general agreement. There were approving glances.

Anjali interjected, "Aren't we rushing it?"

To which Joseph replied, "You're right. These are just our first thoughts on the subject."

Richard continued, "We should begin with his teammates, once we categorize the disciples as subordinates. What did they have to say?

"To help us along, I have flagged pages and underscored passages," Sammy offered.

"We should learn to do our homework like Sammy," Joseph applauded.

"Not only Sammy, but I also have used a highlighter for important passages," George took a spot of glory, as approving smiles greeted him.

"What strikes me about Jesus is his strong conviction," Anjali initiated.

"This reminds me of the words of Robert Townsend of Avis, *'Things get done in our society because of a man or woman with conviction,'* Joseph added, in support of Anjali's statement.

"Unlike most of us buckling under threats or pressure, Jesus stood firm. Threats to his person, ridicule from important people, fear that his disciples would leave him - none of these made Jesus change his beliefs and teaching. His resolve was firm. And his actions reinforced his words. He was consistent; definitely a lesson for us," reasoned Sammy.

"Unquestionably, his maturity stood out," Anjali suggested.

"What would you call maturity?" Sammy interrogated.

"On behalf of Anjali, I'll try to answer that question, but I cannot offer a comprehensive definition. To my mind maturity, is a happy mix of conviction and empathy. The mature person decides and acts with conviction. That quality is judiciously mixed with consideration for other people," Richard came to Anjali's rescue.

"By that standard are we mature?" Lambert asked, fishing for some feedback from Joseph on his appraisal.

"We shall certainly discuss it when we come to our appraisals. For now, let us check on how Jesus measures on the maturity scale." Joseph tactfully answered him. "Was he mature? Did he combine conviction with empathy?" Joseph probed.

"Loads of it," Sammy replied confidently.

"The word 'compassion' is repeated often in the Gospels. We have no doubt, a compassionate person empathizes," Sammy continued with his shop-floor experience.

"The Gospels use the word compassion often. I like to believe the writers really meant empathy. When one has compassion, pity for the plight of the suffering person follows, and there is a desire to offer relief to the one suffering. One tends to lose sight of the receiver's self-respect when pity motivates the act. With empathy, there is a feeling of a higher order.

One tends to identify with the suffering person, one visualizes his feelings and his experience. Put simply, one gets into his shoes. You don't force help; one checks how the person in need wants it.

It's precisely how Jesus acted when anyone came to him for help. He asked the suffering person what he wanted. Only then did he respond; and he responded promptly. Jesus responded the way a suffering person sought help, he empathized with the person. In contrast, what do we do? We extend help grudgingly, take credit for it, and show no concern for the person we tried to help. Did he benefit from the help? It does not concern us." Richard's clear understanding of the point had the team applauding.

"Richard, you picture us as heartless people. That's a fact. Do we really care enough?" Anjali asked with some pain.

"Even those who teased him with awkward questions were not answered in anger. Jesus carefully, and fittingly replied them," George joined in.

"Look at the way he managed his disciples, his team," Sammy added.

"Who were these men? Ordinary fisher folk whom he transformed," he continued.

"He used Situational Management. Not a fixed style, he was always adapting to the situation and the person." Joseph recalled what Lambert had told him a few days ago on the Situational Management style that he was trying to adopt.

"Richard's check-list will have all these points, no doubt," Joseph announced.

"Let us not drift. We'll keep to what we wanted to examine. What his subordinates, the disciples had to say of him," Richard corrected course.

"Richard, we want to stay on course. But since we are freewheeling let our thoughts take us along for a while." Joseph pleaded.

"Right then, what is it going to be?" Richard questioned.

"Look at us, all of us. Our high-priced shoes, expensive branded suits, classy ties, smartphones, computers, credit cards, business-class air travel, stay at five-star hotels and holiday resorts, and bulging wallets; not forgetting our fancy designations and flashy cars - all our props. What would we be without these props? How effective would we be? How would others see us? How would we see ourselves? Chances are that we will be seen as impostors," Joseph challenged his VPs.

There was a pregnant pause as each let his thoughts roam. What would it really look like, bereft of executive trappings? Hollow men in branded clothes, weird.

"Almost naked," Lambert said despondently.

"Naked!" George recoiled at the thought.

"And look at Jesus. He wore the simplest of clothes. No proper place to lodge, wandering gypsy-like from village to village, town to town. Yet he stayed focused, fully focused and he gained respect." Joseph expanded on their thoughts.

"It was a different time, a very different period." Anjali halted Joseph.

"You are right. But think of it. There were others, more ceremoniously dressed, with big titles to their names, plus a horse or a mule for travel. Many had a better living standard and cash to spend. Jesus had none of these, yet he gained more respect than most Pharisees. What was his secret?" Joseph would not let go.

"A fine way of looking at it," Sammy agreed.

"What was his secret?" Joseph repeated.

"His charisma, his character, and his personality were his secrets," Sammy suggested, and continued. "Being sober, dignified and dependable, he built trust. His charisma was such, when he said, 'Follow me', they followed him. Not just the fisherman, but also the tax collector. His personality was consistently mature in different situations."

"He radiated confidence, which came from deep inside. No bravado. He spoke with authority. He was accessible to the poor and the rich. Perhaps those qualities gave him strong, charismatic appeal. He earned their respect and then gained their trust," George expanded.

"Peter Drucker had much to say on character. A person without character destroys. He destroys people, destroys spirit, and destroys performance." Drucker was a favorite with Richard.

"This is why the character of Jesus drew people to him. His character made him stand out among others, the pretenders and the power brokers." Anjali reasoned.

"Yes, that's true," Joseph affirmed.

"So, he stood tall, even without props. We need all our props because we lack his sterling qualities?" Sammy questioned.

"I agree, after reading the Gospels we seem more like pygmies in the presence of a giant," Anjali concluded.

"Can we now get back to his disciples?" Richard sounded impatient.

"Why, were we not discussing Jesus?" Joseph teased.

"Yes, we were but we are now off our agenda," Richard argued.

"We shall now get to the disciples and what they thought of Jesus," Joseph affirmed.

"Not so fast," Sammy interjected. "Joseph, you used the word 'focused', Jesus was focused."

"Yes. I did." Joseph concurred.

"What was his focus?" Sammy demanded.

"He was focused on his mission and therefore his daily work had a purpose and a meaning. Consider his mission. You recall, we read about it in the material we received. It had three parts. The three parts sprang from the main mission. The first part was the ushering in of a new order. An order founded on the love of God and his fellowmen. From this emerged the other two, service to fellowmen and reconciliation with wrong doers. The second and third are sequels to the first. If one had love, the rest followed. Jesus was, all the time, focused on his Mission. He knew why he was here, and he didn't let distractions get in the way. Even when people were impressed with him and wanted to crown him as their King, he declined the high office and remained focused on his mission. What about us? We are seldom focused. The slightest distraction takes us away from our goal and our routine. We earn our wages and put them in wallets with holes in them," Joseph reasoned.

"After reading the Gospels and admiring the qualities of Jesus, our self-worth is taking a beating, don't you think?" queried Sammy.

"Yes. I think so too. I am encouraged by the fact such introspection will help us change and grow. Unless we know our weaknesses, we cannot improve," Joseph agreed.

"Is the love of fellowmen supposed to cover even the opposition?" George shot off at a tangent.

"Yes. When he said, 'love your enemies' he meant it and he showed us how," Joseph explained.

"How would you use it in the marketplace, Lambert?" George pursued.

"Lambert, may I answer that question for you?" Joseph implored.

Lambert looked pleased.

"A tricky question, George. Let's see how it should work, not how it works. My competitor is doing his job, as I am doing mine. For me to hate him and pull him down because he is in the opposite camp is pointless. I might not agree with him, but I don't have to malign him. *'You have to compete and co-operate at the same time.'* Aren't those the words of Raymond Noorda, the former CEO of Novell? For example, we could end up on the same side of the table when our united efforts explain common problems to the Government. Our joint efforts could clear wrong ideas on product categories. We push ourselves to perform better because of our competitors. In other words, we need our competitors for strength. In a way, competition does us a good turn. So, instead of despising them, we should try to understand them. Look at Jesus. The Pharisees and Sadducees and other groups looked for ways to snare him and undermine him. How did he respond? He exposed hypocrisy but, extended a hand in friendship. He faulted deceit, not the deceiver. He accused manipulation, not the manipulator. He begged the sinner not to sin again but forgave the sinner readily. I see no contradiction in his mission and the way he dealt with the opposition. It is a question of understanding the Mission and applying it sensibly to the competition," Joseph replied.

"Great defense, Joseph," commended Lambert. Joseph smiled in acknowledgment.

"If what you say, is the new way we should look at the competition, I am for it., Though I am in finance and not in the marketplace, I see needless hostility. We could do without some of it," Anjali inferred.

"Let our corporation give a lead in pulling down artificial barriers separating us in industry. The market is big enough for all of us to survive and prosper." The leader in Joseph surfaced.

"Would the all-embracing love of Jesus explain his detachment from material possessions? He owned little or nothing. He craved for nothing." Anjali asked.

"Here again we should interpret the passages in the right context. He did not want money or material possessions. He loved his mother. In fact, the first miracle he performed was at her behest. Yet he planned to leave her no material legacy. His attitude to money was rather simple. Money is necessary. It has a role to play. But do not get attached to money, he cautioned. Don't become a slave to money, he admonished. Don't let it become an obsession, he warned. He praised the thrifty. He commended the resourceful and enterprising. He chided wasteful behavior," Joseph expanded.

"What a contrast to the way we see things! For us, stock prices reflect the health of the company. We even twist accounting to manipulate stock prices. Sales and profits tell us how well we are doing. Reserves indicate the security of our future. We are mystified by numbers, not by substance. We are captivated by winning at all costs," George proposed.

"How do we apply it in the corporate world?" Anjali asked.

"Make profits. Yes. We owe it to our company to make justifiable profits, but not profiteering. No cutting corners to make a profit, and no illegal ways of making a profit. With the profits we make we have some social concerns to address. Don't we expect rich nations to help poor nations? In the same way, corporations doing well, have a responsibility to return something to society, not just by way of taxes. In a way, helping society is enlightened self-interest. A more developed society becomes a more responsive market for new products. An improved lifestyle is a fertile ground for planting innovative ideas. Enlightened self-interest apart, we ought to share something with those in need. The examples of Bill Gates and Warren Buffet should inspire us. They make enormous profits but, readily distribute substantial sums in charity. Simply put, fascination with an improving bottom line is good, as long as we are not enslaved by it. It's difficult to follow but try, we shall." Joseph spoke those words with a rare vehemence. He had always held, in public and in private, a corporate citizen had more than ordinary obligations to society.

"Since Jesus was detached from wealth and possessions, he could look at people and circumstances objectively." George proposed.

"True. Take his golden rule. Do unto others as you would have them do to you. This was possible because he was objective and fair. Jesus wasn't affected by labels and he was always sworn to love," added Joseph.

"Is that possible in our corporate situation?" George raised a doubt.

"It is very, very difficult, sometimes almost impossible. Yet it makes sense. I am aware I cannot equate transactions I may have with my chauffeur, to transactions I may have with my suppliers or buyers. There will be a difference. The tragedy today is the total lack of respect for those without proper labels. I quickly adjust to the rank or status of the person in front of me. I respond to a label. What I need to do is to realize that behind each label, big or small, is a person. Each person begs to be treated with dignity. Our harsh response leads to hurt feelings. Our double standards are exposed. Jesus pleaded that we do away with our double standards." Joseph was persuasive.

"Perhaps that is why Jesus did not abuse his power," Anjali deduced.

"To begin with, we should try to understand what we mean by power and authority. Some experts define power as the ability to influence the beliefs and actions of others, and authority, as the right to make decisions affecting others. Take Jesus. He had enormous power. He worked wondrous deeds and communicated effectively. His knowledge was praised. His power was seen time and again but, did he abuse power? People were following him in droves, yet it was always *'if you believe'* and *'your faith has made you whole,'* it wasn't about him, but them. No pressure, not even subtle pressure to convert. With his powers, he could have performed miracles when he was arrested and taken before the high priests and Pilate. To save himself he could have performed the magic they were waiting for and stunned his audience. No; he would not use cheap gimmicks. He believed in placing facts before people, expecting them to decide, without a trace of compulsion. No, he did not use his enormous powers to influence people to his thinking. Real power is when you have it and restrain yourself from using it; be prudent and empathetic in exercising it. And of his authority, we see disciplined use. He asked his disciples to follow a particular code. When they failed, he was gentle and forgiving. With others it was always, *'what would you want me to do for you?'* The option rested with the other person. Jesus responded when they chose an option or made a request. His authority was never oppressive. You are right Anjali; Jesus did not abuse his power. We have only to look at the way we transact, to admire Jesus. We exercise the little power we have with a sense of bravado. We want people to fear us because we have some power. And our display of authority is almost vulgar. But we are quick to bow before someone in higher authority. Our use of power and authority is a sham." Richard was emphatic.

George was ready with the next question: "As I read the four Gospels, a question puzzled me, why didn't Jesus marry and raise a family like Rabbis of his time or some of his disciples?"

Joseph offered to answer him. "There's a difficult question but, I'll try to answer it. Jesus should have had good reasons for staying single. The Gospels do not provide us with any reasons for his choice. We can make some assumptions, based on his personality and mission. One, Jesus knew his life was short. Leaving behind a young wife and perhaps tiny children did not seem a good option to someone full of empathy. Two, his work took him from place to place. He could not settle in one town. He could not sink roots. His family, if he had one, would suffer from neglect. Even his mother, whom he loved dearly, could rarely spend time with him. Three, his mission was his prime focus. If he took on family responsibilities his mission-efforts would receive less time and attention. Four, he was not in a job or profession which gave him earnings. He had given up his work as a carpenter to make time for his mission. With no income, his family would be put to unending financial difficulty. As a wandering rabbi, he depended on the generosity of his followers and listeners to keep body and soul together. Five, the Gospels portray him as the Son of God. An earthly family would not fit his Divine program. I am not sure, but I believe our assumptions could be the reasons why Jesus chose to remain single. It appears he did not want to start a relationship he could not nurture. He was careful not to take on anything he could not complete."

"Thank you, Joseph. Your assumptions are logical," said George.

"As a staunch Hindu, I have something to share with you. Recently, I read an enlightening book titled, *Divine Harmony* by Aravindaksha Menon, a Vedic scholar. He makes a strong case for Jesus, with the help of the Vedas or Hindu Scripture, as his source. We all know the Vedas emerged from seers between 2600 and 1500 BC, before Jesus was born and the Gospels were written. Verse 7, of chapter 90, of the 10th book, the Rigveda, states: *'At the time of the sacrifice, the Son of God, called Prajapathy, will be tightly tied to a wooden sacrificial post, by his hands and legs, using iron nails. He will bleed to death, and on the third day he will regain life in the resurrection.'* Praja means man and Pathy means savior. So, Jesus was the savior of man, as stated in the Rigveda. Many verses in the Vedas match those in the Gospels, including that on a virgin giving birth to Jesus. They also refer to the many healings he would perform." Sammy contribution had the team in awe.

Anjali added: "Sammy, I have not read the book you cited, but Selections from Swamy Vivekananda. I was edified to read one of Vivekananda's quotations on page 411: *'I am from the Orient. If I adore Jesus Christ, I have only one way – worship him as my God, no way else.'* Those words from a Hindu, like me, set me thinking. Jesus, as the Son of God, is not a dimension we will be discussing in our meetings but, it is something worth pondering."

On hearing the two Hindus speak, Joseph connected: "Now, you have given me more substance to the argument I made on Gandhi, a Hindu, reading the Gospels and liking them."

Lambert's handphone buzzed, it was Lissy. The day went well at her brother's place, they had a grand celebration and they all missed him. They were leaving by the night train and would be in on Monday morning. Augustus wanted to say hello to daddy. When the call was over, Lambert checked his watch. It was ten past one.

Ravi fetched some short eats and drinks. The sight of food and drink was refreshing. Breaking off from the serious discussion, they teased Joseph on his weight gain and suggested he join a Gym or at least jog. He promised to start jogging but, disliked the idea of the Gym.

George asked Joseph if he planned to continue the discussion in the afternoon. He was willing to stay on; but what about the others? Since none of the others had engagements in the afternoon, they all decided to continue with the discussions, at least until 3:30 or 4 pm.

When the trolley was cleared, Richard cleared his throat and declared officially: "We shall now get down to what the disciples had to say." The group went into a fit of laughter.

"Why do we have to rush?" Joseph inquired of Richard.

"I was beginning to wonder whether we would get back at all," Richard was not amused.

"Richard is right. Now we stick to the 360-degree appraisal for Jesus. Let us hear what the disciples had to say," Joseph was enthusiastic.

"Thomas said they (the disciples) should go and die with Jesus. Peter asked Jesus where else they could go but to him. Peter also declared they had left everything and followed him. Mathew gave up his job as a tax collector to follow Jesus. Each showed a readiness to accept his leadership; to obey him and to accept correction. He offered them no money, no fame, only *'take up your cross and follow me'* and they followed." George had read the Gospels in full and could marshal facts.

"What we are trying to say is, his Team Management skills were of a high order and feedback from the team was edifying," Sammy concluded.

"We are then agreed, in the third quadrant we put down, 'very good'," Richard tossed the idea in the open. "Since the 360-degree appraisal focuses on relationships, and we are examining the possibility of setting up Jesus as a Model for our relationships, we shall have to review our assessments and appraisal as we learn more of him," Joseph was cautious.

"What did his peers have to say?" Sammy asked.

"John the Baptist, Nicodemus, Joseph of Arimathea, the Centurion and Zacchaeus are seen as important peers. Since they held important positions in society, their statements should throw some light. Each one treated Jesus with great respect and admiration," George had his facts right.

"Don't we see any discord, for example, from the High priests?" Anjali challenged.

"The High priests were, no doubt, people in high positions, however, they had vested interests. Jesus was attracting crowds and creating a sensation. The High priests felt threatened. Naturally, they would not speak kindly of the man they feared. One cannot be influenced by what they had to say. The close attention they paid to the feedback they got on him, if at all, can be seen as a grudging tribute paid to Jesus," George reasoned.

"The enlightened and fair-minded peers had only good things to say of Jesus?" Richard asked pointedly.

"Yes, exactly," said George, very decisively.

"In which case, what comment shall we put down in quadrant two, against peers?" Richard asked, ready to takedown points.

"Let it be 'very good'," Joseph suggested. "As I said earlier, we shall review this later. For now, let us retain 'very good' unless someone has a strong reason to give it a different mark."

Lambert looked at the others.

They shrugged their shoulders and decided to go along. So, it stayed as 'very good' with the appropriate elaboration Richard would give it.

"The fourth relationship is perhaps the most important. How did the customers see him?"

This question should have come from Lambert, the marketing man, instead it came from the finance person, Anjali.

"Those who were influenced by the opposite camp chose to make derogatory statements. The others had only praise for Jesus. They praised his gentle ways, marveled at his great deeds, were amazed at his new teaching, and his communication skills cast a spell on them," Joseph glowed.

"Those he came to serve are seen as his customers. And feedback from them is positive, very positive. Only those who tried to trap him in the debate had caustic remarks to pass, more because they could not match him and failed to expose him. So, what hesitation do we have in putting down remarks in the fourth quadrant?" Sammy was impatient.

"No hesitation, what do you say, Lambert?" Joseph queried.

"What is fine by you is fine by me," Lambert was feebly courteous.

Joseph looked at him and looked away, something was wrong, he thought.

"Shall we put down 'very good' in that space?" Richard asked.

"Yes, 'very good' it shall be." Joseph bellowed.

Richard looked at his pad and said: "Let's quickly look at the remarks we have given Jesus in each quadrant of the 360-degree appraisal format. Under 'superiors' in the first quadrant, we have 'positive.' Under 'peers' in the second also we have 'positive.' Under 'subordinates' in the third, we have 'very positive.' The fourth quadrant, under 'customers' we also have 'very positive.'

This is not final, only our initial reaction. I shall work on this, fill in the blanks, and expand points where necessary. But if the overall assessment meets with your approval, I shall take it as approved," Richard was trying to get his summary cleared.

Heads shook in vigorous agreement.

"May we call it a day?" Anjali enquired. She had to drive a long way to her place.

"Yes but, this is not the end. Remember, we have to prepare for Lambert's Marketing Conference, in the next few days. We have much to learn from Jesus and apply those lessons to our situation. Now let us get back to our families and enjoy what is left of our Sunday." Joseph concluded.

Chapter Eleven: Sink or Sail Together

"For they can conquer, who believe they can." Virgil.

Monday was another fast-paced day. At Lambert's desk, his smartphone had been buzzing right through the day. It was 5 o'clock and it buzzed again.

Irked, Lambert picked up the phone, planning to dismiss the caller abruptly. It was Joseph on the line and Lambert's mood changed instantly.

Joseph: "How busy are you this evening?"
Lambert: "Why? Tell me."
Joseph: "Can you set aside an hour?"
Lambert: "Yes."
Joseph: "If that is okay by you. Tell Ravi to take your car home. Be my guest. I'll give you a drop home."
Lambert: "Is there anything in particular that you wish to discuss?"
Joseph: "Yes. You and I need to chat for a while."
Joseph: "I'll be ready at 5:55. Does that suit you?"
Joseph: "Okay."

As he settled in his chair, Lambert wondered what the problem could be. What was the 'chat' about? Could it be his appraisal? Or was someone back-stabbing? He put such thoughts aside, dispatched Ramona at 5:30. Then spent his time going through papers he would discuss at the Marketing Managers and Regional Managers Meeting on Thursday and Friday.

Joseph looked in at 5:55 and they stepped out together. There was no talk as they went down to the car park. Joseph held the car door open for Lambert, then took the wheel and eased his white Audi out of the car park in silence. Joseph drove slowly as the melody from Strauss' Blue Danube filled the car. Lambert looked at him for a hint, but there was none. They pulled up at the parking lot near the beach, got out of the car and began walking towards the University Campus. Lambert was waiting for a clue. What was Joseph up to?

To put an end to the tension, Lambert asked: "Joseph, what did you have in mind?"

"Lambert, I am glad you asked," he paused, wrung his hands, and continued, "When we met at your place on Sunday, I found you rather withdrawn. Apathetic is too strong, perhaps aloof and disinterested are more appropriate. The others were involved, you were not. Why?"

"Are you suggesting I was not a caring host?"

"You know what I mean, we spent time discussing Jesus and you seemed distant. Why?"

"Perhaps, I had very little to contribute."

"Tell that to the Marines, I know you well enough; something was wrong."

"I was not in my usual form, perhaps."

"Don't kid me."

"Joseph, this discussion on Jesus makes me very uncomfortable."

"Of all people you to be uncomfortable with Jesus. Why?"

"No. I am not uncomfortable with Jesus. It's just that I cannot see him in our situation. I cannot think of him being dragged into our corporate world. What do we have except pretensions, deceit, the chasing of money and fame and the driving of people to achieve our money goals? We are crazed with sales and more sales, profits and more profits. Jesus is God. I cannot have him mixed up with the corporate world."

"Let me try to understand, you believe Jesus is God. I won't challenge your belief because I share the same belief. Be assured, we are not assaulting or assailing his Divine Personality. I made the point clear at the start. As Christians, we see his Divinity. As humans, we see him and his sterling qualities. We are not into confusing the two parts. None of us would confuse the two sides of his being or question any Divine attribute. What exactly do you fear?"

"Joseph, try to understand me. From my early childhood, my mother taught me to love and respect Jesus as my God. I have accepted him as God, and he will stay that way. I cannot tamper with my belief. I cannot change my mindset."

"For heaven's sake, Lambert, be reasonable. Who is suggesting you change your mindset? All we are saying is look at the man, the person. Is there something for us to learn from the person?"

"Joseph, we have people like Jack Welch, Bill Gates, and our own Ratan Tata. Let us try to figure out what kind of models they are, let us learn from them."

"Have no doubts, Lambert, we will. As professionals, we shall look everywhere to find answers to our questions. Our approach takes us to Jesus. Perhaps Jesus has different lessons to teach us. Not the ones we've learned from Jack Welch and Bill Gates."

"Joseph, is this really necessary? To me, it's a traumatic experience. It's like combining the sublime with the sordid. Our corporate world leaves much to be desired."

"Precisely, the very reason we need models to help us change and improve. We need someone to transcend our petty lapses and grave indiscretions. We need to study the Gospels to find Jesus the model, the towering model."

"Are you suggesting we can find no other model? No other person to follow?"

"No, I see a strong option in Jesus. Frankly, at any time during our discussions did we show disrespect to the person of Jesus? Anjali said High Priests were not among his admirers. Sammy said some of his customers tried to trap him in discourse. I found nothing offending in those remarks. Those comments were not made to offend, but to state the fact."

"I am not accusing anyone of showing disrespect, I am just uncomfortable with the idea."

"Why did you agree to host the meeting at your home, when you had such reservations?"

"Remember, I told you I am a team player. The needs of my team come first. Despite my discomfort with the subject, I put the interest of the team ahead of my feelings."

An uneasy pause followed. They walked for some distance without speaking a word, until Joseph asked: "Lambert, have you spoken with Lissy?"

"Briefly. No, not yet."

"Why don't you? Perhaps she has some input and I am ready to listen."

"I can talk to her."

"Will you do me two favors?"

"Yes, I'm always happy to help."

"Talk to Lissy tonight. Tell me about it tomorrow morning. Also, since we both believe Jesus is God, raise your heart to him. Talk to him. Tell him what we are about, then get back to me. Can you do me these favors?"

"Yes, certainly I will do both of them."

"Like the night watchman who expectantly waits for the break of dawn, I am going to wait for your reply." Quoting from Scripture, Joseph could not have concluded more fittingly.

They stopped at the soft drink parlor and grabbed two cans. As they walked back to the car finishing their drinks, Lambert seemed less stressed and Joseph intuitively knew Lissy, his wife, and Jesus, his God, would resolve his doubts.

On Tuesday morning, Joseph was in his office early, even before Olivia. He had to plan for his upcoming trip to Singapore. Then he prepared points for his interaction with the Marketing Managers and the Regional Managers during the upcoming conference on Thursday and Friday. He had some emails to check and wanted to find ways of getting his VP's together for an 'idea' launch during the conference. There was much to be done this week.

Olivia barged in and was surprised to see her boss in his office earlier than usual. She did not see his car in the parking lot, because his driver had taken the car home for Teresa. She came back with his usual coffee and asked if she could help. "Olivia, I am sure you have lined up things for my Singapore Trip. Just go over all the arrangements. No matter what, if VP Marketing calls, put him through to me."

Joseph was left alone with his thoughts. Richard met him at home, late on Monday night, to brief him on the work he had done. On Monday, after meeting each of the VPs separately he made sense of their general observations and statements. He had handled the whole exercise splendidly.

What would we do without Richard, he thought? Even as Joseph was lost in his thoughts, Olivia tiptoed into his office.

"VP Marketing is waiting to meet you, are you ready for him?"

"Of course, send him in immediately."

Lambert walked in. The grey stripes on his maroon tie, against his light grey shirt, looked striking. Tall, handsome, well dressed, this fellow could make a lot of heads turn, Joseph thought. He grabbed Lambert by the hand and motioned him to a chair.

"Lissy and I talked, and I prayed."

"Good, thank you, Lambert." Joseph waited expectantly.

"There is some sense in what she says," he paused. "She says I have to look beyond what I am doing now. Put simply, she says the more depraved the situation, the greater the need for a loftier model. Since the sins of the corporate world will haunt us, we need a towering personality, an unmatched and powerful model, to exorcise those demons. Despite some great ones, most men have feet of clay. They are imperfect models. After all, it is only the great personality of Jesus we are examining. Not his Divinity. Come to think of it, his qualities are unmatched. He is peerless in forging and strengthening relationships. I did not sleep well last night. I kept thinking of what you and Lissy had to say. I prayed, again and again: *"Lead kindly light, lead"*.

It was only after three this morning I dozed off and I felt a lot better this morning. Sorry, I did not call you before coming. I gatecrashed since I did not want to keep you in suspense." Joseph put up his hand to stop any further expressions of regret.

"Joseph, I'm sorry. I guess, I was a little closed to the idea. I didn't mean to cause you distress. It's a good thing we discussed it. You didn't leave me wallowing in my own thoughts. I'm glad you challenged me."

Joseph understood Lambert had been through a harrowing night. It explained his disjointed statements. He understood Lambert's predicament and captured the essence of his rambling conversation.

Thankfully, the crux made sense. He did not tell him that he had voiced the same thoughts that Lissy had. It wasn't his style.

"Lambert, the watchman's vigil is over, and I have not watched in vain. The break of dawn has brought me good news. Thank you. I was worried you might turn out to be the lone voice against the idea. I was counting on your support and you were shooting off at a tangent. You know, with us, it is simply sink or sail together. I was puzzled. Richard has done a great job putting things together but, we would have been beaten before we began if you weren't with us. Imagine, talking to the Marketing Managers and Regional Managers without the support of their VP?"

"Yes, that would have been tough on you." Lambert was sheepish.

"All's well that ends well," Joseph added joyously.

"What's next?" Lambert asked.

"It will be Friday's concluding session. You had invited Mr. Das, our consultant, to address your team. We shall cancel his participation and reschedule it for another time. This Friday afternoon it will be in-house inputs. I'll kick start it. Richard will handle the session with your active support. Remember: Jesus said a good tree does not bear bad fruit. Ours is a good tree, great idea. Let us taste the feedback fruit our managers give us on Friday afternoon."

Chapter Twelve: The Need to Change

"I want to change things. I want to see things happen. I don't want just to talk about them." J.K. Galbraith.

After much preparation by the presenters, and great anticipation in the participants, the special session was to start at 2:05 pm on Friday. Joseph D'cruz, the Chief Executive, walked into the Conference Hall. A sudden hush fell over the group of managers assembled for their review meeting. For a day and a half, they labored over figures and strategies, over tactics and promotional offers. This afternoon was to be different; they would discuss ideas removed from targets and deadlines.

In the Summit room, seated around the conference table, were Richard Rozario, Lambert Kurien, Anjali Kelkar, Sammy Ghosh, and George Ferns, the five Vice Presidents. Also present was Raphael Mathew, Sunil Vachani, and Laxmi Ramanathan, the three Marketing Managers, reporting directly to Lambert Kurien. And, the six Regional Managers Latif Basha, Manju Kaul, Jordan David, Jonathan Lobo, Muthukrishnan Iyer, and Marcela D'Monte, reporting to Marketing Managers.

India was divided into five regions, the sixth Regional Manager, Marcela, oversaw exports. It was not a big segment of company revenue but, there were hopes of enlarging the operation. She was not known for her fashionable clothes, more for her sharp comprehension, ready wit, and hands-on performance. She reveled in honing her skills in communication. She would rather read a book on English usage than attend a fashion show. Not all of these managers attended business school, some moved up to their current positions by working their way up from field jobs in Sales. Many were savvy in their functions but were not abreast of management thinking. This afternoon, the top team hoped to bridge the gap, a little. A summit conference at Mount Pharmaceuticals was about to begin with 15 high ranking managers in the conference hall.

The Chief Executive stood up, looked around and began rather slowly, "Ladies and gentlemen, you are here for the customary Review Meeting. You have interacted with the VP Marketing. I have no doubt that you had a rewarding day-and-a-half of deliberations. Later, I shall discuss the meeting with Mr. Lambert Kurien. I'm not going to touch on any of the points already covered. I am here for a different purpose. I said you are here for the customary Review Meeting. I must correct myself. This is not customary. It should not be customary. Each review meeting should be different, special. I assure you, this meeting will be different and special. The Vice Presidents and I have discussed a few new ideas. Human Resources, Vice President, Mr. Richard Rozario, will place these new ideas before the house. Mr. Kurien will step in where necessary, as will the other Vice Presidents. I am here, just to let you know, the afternoon session is of tremendous importance to you and to our company. We want your initial response to these ideas. Normally, in such meetings, questioning is subverted and systematically shut down. Let it not be so in this meeting. Foster a questioning attitude, it promotes better brainstorming. Please feel free to voice your thoughts. Please realize that we do value your opinions. It's the reason we planned this session. I shall leave now but shall return before you conclude. I wish you a stimulating discussion and I thank you for your participation." There was silence as the CEO left the conference room.

Richard Rozario moved to the top of the table. Behind him was the screen for his power point presentation and to his right, the whiteboard on which he would write down some points. He smiled warmly at his audience and ensured good eye contact. He began, "Ladies and gentlemen, I welcome you to an afternoon of brainstorming, where the focus will be more on your questions than on our answers. With the Chief, I wish you an enjoyable afternoon. Let me begin with a short story. It's an adapted version of a legend, used by Shiv Khera in one of his books. The words of the characters are mine. It is early afternoon. The wise old man of a village is sitting under a big tree. A traveler stops by and addresses the old man.

"Uncle, could you tell me about the people of your village?"

"Why would you want to know about the people of our village?" The old man inquires.

"I am having trouble at my village. I wish to move out to another village and find some work." the stranger replies.

"I shall certainly tell you about the people in this village. Before that, will you tell me about the people in your village?" The old man's experience showed.

"The less said the better. The people in my village are rude, mean, quarrelsome and foul-mouthed. They are evil!" he hisses.

"Sadly, the people in this village are the same. They are evil." As he said this, the old man looked pensive. The stranger shakes his head and walks down the road.

The next afternoon, the old man is again at his favorite spot.

Another traveler stops and asks him: "Uncle, could you please advise me? I want to shift out of my village to another village. Where I am, I do not have much work. I am trying to find a village where I can get some work and where people are kind. Are people in this village kind?"

The old man says, Tell me about the people in your village".

"Oh! They are just wonderful, so helpful. They do not want me to move out, but unless I find work, my family will starve. I have no doubt the people will help me, but I cannot accept help every day. So, I must find work in a new place, where I am welcome'.

The old man is silent for a long time. Then he says, "Finding work here is not going to be difficult. We have big farmers, looking to hire hands. The people here are wonderful, very helpful.' The stranger smiles, he thanks the old man and promises to return. That is the end of the story."

Richard looked around. He noticed that his audience was trying to grapple with the different responses of the old man.

"What do you think is the moral of the story?" Richard asked.

Jonathan, eager to participate, ventured: "Good and bad are relative. There are no absolutes."

"Can you explain your comments?" Richard pushed.

"What he meant to say, if you look through colored glasses, you see things colored." Marcela interrupted.

"Thank you, Marcela, but let him try to explain," Richard urged.

"Marcela spoke well," Jonathan promptly agreed with his colleague.

"I think this is a clear case of how perceptions matter. How perceptions are different and how they affect people," Sunil pointed out.

"Are you trying to say we see things not the way they are, but the way we are? The first traveler thought evil and he found evil. The second traveler looked for good and he found good. The old man was trying to say: if you look at people with fellow feeling, you will find friendship. Looking at things with clear eyes and looking at things with jaundiced eyes makes a difference!"

"Well said," Sunil complimented Richard.

"Thank you, Sunil, you are kind," Richard said and continued, "Are we agreed on the moral of the story? "There were reaffirming nods. "As we go along, we shall find the moral of this story has a bearing on the points to follow, our perceptions matter."

"Let me ask you a question: In our context, who is a professional? What is our perception of one?" There was a twinkle in Richard's eyes as he placed the posers before them. There was silence since they were afraid to say anything stupid.

Laxmi broke the silence, "In very simple terms, a professional is one who manages her resources. These could be products, markets, trade, cash, and people. She tries to maximize her returns from the resources."

Richard looked at her approvingly and said: "Yes, there are several definitions in management books. We are not going to spend our time discussing them. We are not writing examinations or appearing for interviews. What we want to examine are our perceptions."

Raphael added, "I think Laxmi gave us the crux. I might want to change the term "maximize" to effectively manage."

"So, you say the word maximize has hidden dangers. Effective management is a happy blend of all kinds of effort," Richard suggested.

"Yes. When you want to maximize results from one resource, the results from another could get compromised. Effective management means to maintain a balance." Raphael explained.

"Management is, therefore, not a matter of answers or solutions but a precarious balancing act.' Those are the words of Stuart Grainer who writes in 'Business, the Jack Welch Way'," George added.

"To perform this balancing act, the professional must have knowledge and skills," Manju elaborated.

"What about his attitudes and beliefs?" Latif challenged, and added, "A study done at Harvard University showed 85 percent of the time, a person gets a job or a promotion because of his attitude, and only 15 percent due to his education, qualification, and skill."

Richard took the cue and amplified, "Shiv Khera is reported to have said that his interactions with Chief Executives in different parts of the world have thrown up one factor - Attitude. They tell him, the most important factor affecting productivity, profits, and teamwork is attitude." Latif was elated with the support he got from Richard and nodded his appreciation.

"A professional must effectively manage the resources he has or procures. He must have the requisite knowledge, skills, habits, and attitude," said Richard.

Both Jordan and Marcela started out at once, but Jordan managed to put his thought across, "To me, that seems fine, but the conditions in which he operates will help or hinder his progress. For example, if he works for a company where there is a lack of encouragement, his performance could suffer despite other strong points."

"I agree with Jordan," Marcela echoed.

"So, a professional must learn to cope with circumstances, not in his control?" Richard looked at Jordan and Marcela.

Muthukrishnan did not like being left out, "How can he manage things outside his control?"

"Correct me, if I am wrong, but I recall suggesting a manager must learn to cope with, and not manage, factors outside his control," Richard clarified.

"He must have the resilience to cope with several pressures, task-generated, people-generated, and situation-generated," Marcela expanded. She knew what she was saying because, in the export market, the pressures she has to cope with were often outside her control.

"In other words, his attitudes will cover a wide range, including coping with such situations," Laxmi intoned.

"Why are you leaving out his knowledge and skills?" Manju questioned.

"Please yourself, have them all." Laxmi chuckled.

"Why not one of you summarize the points we have just covered?" Richard requested.

Raphael looked around, "May I?" he asked.

There were approving smiles.

"A professional is first a person. He must never forget that he has his limitations, so he must not stop learning. To learn, he must be open. To effectively manage his resources, which could either be big and diverse or small and limited, he must have adequate knowledge. He must, above all else, keep in mind the good of the company. Good work habits and staying organized are also important. He has to remain positive, optimistic, friendly, and respectful. Good communication and interpersonal skills are vital."

There was spontaneous applause when he finished.

"Raphael, you spoke well. I liked your clarity of thought." Richard commended, and quickly put up a slide.

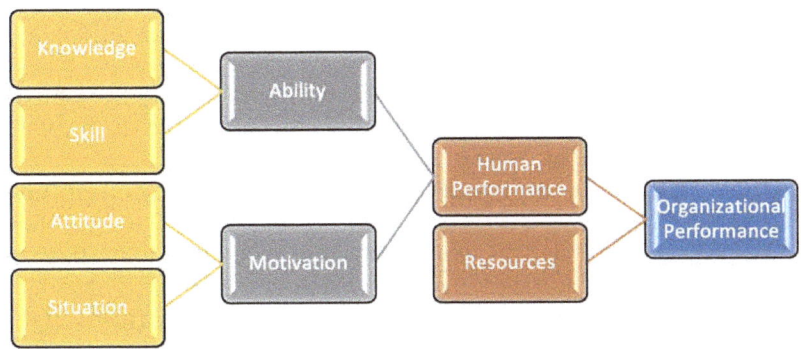

"What Raphael was trying to tell us is summed up in this slide", Richard said. He noticed all writing down what was on the slide.

"I would like to add that he must be seen as a competent professional. Unless he learns to interact successfully with those in his team and those on the outside, his competence is dented. He will have to learn to perform well on his own and raise the level of team-performance to ensure a high standard of achievement. Starting and sustaining happy relationships is a professional quality. Most of us are still learning about it."

"Now that we have some thoughts on the subject, we shall put it on hold for a while. I promise you, we shall return to it," announced Richard.

"We said perceptions matter and those perceptions color our thinking. To change ourselves, we must change our perceptions." Richard looked for a reaction and there was overall approval.

"The question to my mind is, should we change at all? Why not continue the way we are? Are there compelling reasons for us to change?" Richard challenged.

Latif, who had been silent for some time, took up the challenge: "I believe change is the only thing that is certain; every facet of life changes. We are not who we were last year, and next year, I am certain we will not be who we are this year."

"If change is a must, as Latif eloquently explained, then we must decide in what areas we need to change. One tool that helps us is our Appraisal. We are familiar with the tool we use now. The question before us is: Is the way we do our Appraisal right?" Richard let the question sink.

"For now, our boss does the appraisal with us. You don't think it's complete?" Jordan demanded.

"I am not saying so, I am asking the house. Do we think it is adequate? Should we, for example, get to know what our peers have to say about us?" Richard was testing the waters.

"How can our peers comment on us? Only the boss should evaluate us," Jordan was emphatic.

"Don't we transact with our peers? Don't we have a relationship with them? When the relationship is good, aren't we able to gain their support in getting things done?" Richard inquired.

"Yes, it helps. But how can they get involved in the appraisal?" Jordan was anxious.

"Are we afraid of the consequences? Do we fear our poor performances will get noticed, even by our peers?" Richard asked.

"Fear of a wrong interpretation by them is real," Muthukrishnan admitted.

"When the feedback is positive from peers, doesn't it add to our confidence?" Richard angled.

"Yes, it does," Manju answered.

"To ensure we get positive feedback from our peers, we have to perform well. Perhaps change some of our ways. Perhaps pressure ourselves to change," Richard deduced.

"You are coming around to the need for change," Marcela commented.

"Precisely, we all have to change. We have to set ourselves high standards and welcome feedback from our peers. Why we even need input from our subordinates and customers because we work with all of them and we need to build relationships with them," Richard expanded on the logic.

Jordan wished to interrupt, but Richard begged him to wait and continued.

"One writer sums up the idea in this way, all functions are people related. What he meant was, we don't manage a company. We manage people. Mr. Godrej, the noted Indian Industrialist, echoed the same thought when he said, *'All corporate strengths are dependent on people'*."

Then turning to Jordan he said, "Jordan, did you wish to say something?"

"Subordinates, no way, how can we let our subordinates appraise us? The idea is preposterous." Jordan was both loud and indignant.

"Would you like to know that your subordinates think well of you? Do you want them to think that you are fair-minded and that you set a good example?" Richard pitched.

"Yes. I would love to hear that, but not through an Appraisal," Jordan defended.

"Why? Are we terrified at the prospect? Take a look at our interactions in our work situations. We are interacting with a network of seniors, juniors, peers and external agencies. This includes Customers, Suppliers, Traders, Advertising Agencies, Transporters, Bankers, and others. The nature of our interactions determines the success of those relations. When we work well together, we build good relationships that lead to good performances. Do we follow the logic?" Richard commented, as he put up the next slide.

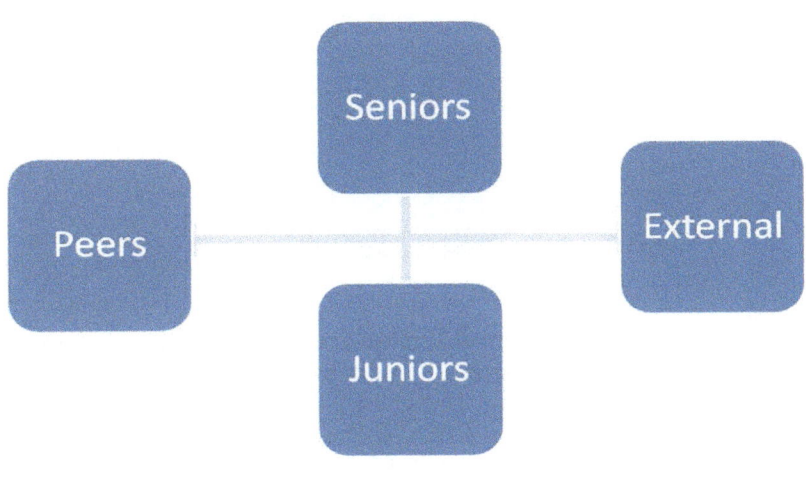

"A performing professional should have no fears. He knows what he has to do and does it. The opinions of others should interest him, not disturb him. Chances are, those opinions will be positive because he is a good professional." Lambert spoke for the first time. So far it was VP Human Resources engaging them in a discussion. Now it was their Head speaking. They listened intently. There was a finality to his words.

"Since we are performing professionals, we have little to fear from any source. Only non-performers are weighed down by such fears. For us, the boss, the peer, the subordinate, or even the customer, should have good things to say, because we perform," Richard reinforced Lambert's comments.

"In a way, what you say is right. I suppose it's just the resistance to change, inherent in us. The gate of change can only be opened from the inside. Right now, we're reluctant to open the gate," Laxmi confessed.

"You're right, Laxmi, that is why we are trying to get each of you involved in the process. Diane Gherson, the Head of HR at IBM, said, *'People are much less likely to resist change when they have a hand in shaping it.'*"

"We know an Appraisal from different people can throw up some points we hadn't considered. People are uncomfortable with the element of surprise," Jonathan added another dimension to Laxmi's admission.

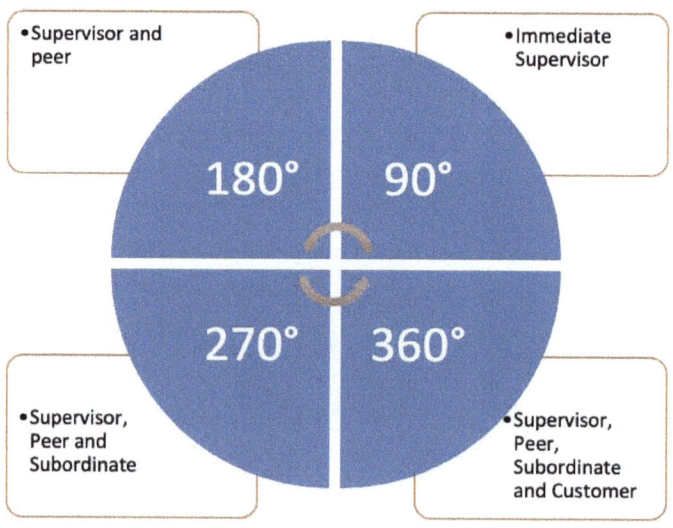

"Granted. Your point is valid. If we are focused on improvement, in time, the surprise elements should be behind us. We will have acted on them and improved on them. Doesn't the professional have to be open to change, starting with himself? In the final analysis, what we are, communicates far more eloquently than anything we say or do " Richard added calmly, borrowing the idea from Stephen R. Covey.

"Mr. Rozario, could you please get to the point? You have teased us all afternoon," Raphael entreated. There was laughter all around.

"My intention was never to tease you, Raphael," Richard explained smiling broadly, "It was to draw you out, and, if possible, to gain a consensus for a new idea."

"Now that I have your attention, I wish to place before you the 360-degree Appraisal. It's a new tool in the Indian context, and it's something totally new to us at Mount Pharmaceuticals." He expanded as he put the next slide on the screen.

Some of them were acquainted with the tool through sessions in business school. The others had questioning looks on their faces. They tried to figure out the illustration, each busy with his own thoughts.

"As of now, we only have the 90-degree appraisal. Each of us is evaluated by his immediate supervisor, with some comments from the boss of the immediate supervisor. For Regional Managers, the appraisal is done by the Marketing Manager. The Vice President Marketing, if necessary, makes a few points in the appraisal form. As a first step, we propose a planned shift to the 180-degree appraisal, with peers submitting feedback on one another. For example, a Regional Manager will also get feedback from the other Regional Managers. This will give the appraisal a new dimension. In stages, we shall move to the 270-degree, where subordinates are invited to share their thoughts, and finally to the 360-degree, where the customer is consulted. The 360-degree appraisal will provide the sum total of feedback from four segments. The traditional method is subjective, often based on the relationship between the individual and his or her immediate supervisor. In the new system, the boss is more like a judge. The multi-source feedback is like a jury looking at the means adopted by the individual to get results. The jury submits findings to the boss before the verdict is pronounced by him. He will continue to judge results and will remain the final authority. He has a chance to check other opinions. In this way, the system improves on the traditional method. It is also important to remember the company looks for trends and patterns, not flashes of brilliance or outstanding performance. When we reach the 360-degree Appraisal, some of the areas that will be spotlighted are: Vision, Pursuit of Excellence, Sense of Accountability, and Empowerment. You will notice these are key qualities to top management. Someone showing improving trends in these areas is well on his way up the company ladder." Richard paused, watching carefully, for reactions. Nobody spoke.

"Esso, in the 1950s, kick-started the appraisal system. Assessments were then on traits, behavior, comparisons, psychological analysis, and ranking. What emerged from the appraisal was feedback on talents, behavior, values, ethical standards, loyalty, and related points. Through stages, the 360-degree appraisal was formally initiated by GE in 1992.

It has several advantages:

1) It tries to assess the candidate's knowledge of industry, company, and job.

2) In terms of effectiveness – quality and quantity – what is the level of his/her performance?

3) Communication skills, time-management, and interpersonal skills come under the radar.

4) The system helps chart the career path of the executive.

5) The 360-degree appraisal helps spot red flags not visible to the manager or supervisor.

6) The system must fit the culture of the company.

Even after he wrote the six points on the board, there was no reaction from the group, so Richard continued, "Some companies in India are ahead of us. We have been slow to change and it's time we caught up with our contemporaries.

The way I see it, there are compelling reasons for using the 360-degree evaluation.

1) How else can we assess improving performance?

2) What methods could we use to ascertain the development needs of the person?

3) How shall we cultivate deeper relationships between and among the boss and colleagues?

4) How can we raise the self-esteem of each in the team?

In my experience in the UK, I can confidently state, an honest conversation between the evaluated employee, his or her boss, and his or her colleagues is a great way of getting answers to the questions we just raised."

He paused again, on purpose, yet there was no comment. And then he threw them the direct challenge: "Are we ready for such a change? We are comfortable with what we know, but fearful of what we do not know." Some shifted in their chairs. Others looked away. The pause was long.

"How soon do you plan to start the new system?" Jonathan asked nervously.

"How soon do you think? Would the next appraisal be okay with you?" Richard inquired.

"Okay by me," Manju declared.

"Me too," Marcela joined in. The rest looked at Manju and Marcela suspiciously.

"So, we are agreed: first, to introduce the 180-degree appraisal when the next appraisals are due. Next, we shall progressively move to the 270-degree and 360-degree appraisal, based on the success we have with the 180-degree," Richard summarized.

Yes, Mr. Rozario," Lambert said. "And thank you. You had us keep on our thinking caps."

"Thank you, Mr. Kurien," Richard replied warmly.

A fifteen-minute break gave them a chance to stretch and compare notes. Tea and short eats made the rounds as everyone broke up into small groups, discussing the proposed changes to their appraisals.

The Chief was right, it was a different meeting.

Chapter Thirteen: The Change Agent

"We are not human beings having a spiritual experience. We are spiritual beings having a human experience." Teilhard de Chardin.

The afternoon session had set minds racing. The new systems that were in the offing did not appeal to everyone. How were they going to fend off negative feedback in the appraisal system? What would happen if the feedback was damaging? Could peers be trusted to give favorable remarks? There were too many thoughts crowding their minds and too little time to address them. So, after tea, when they reassembled for the session, they were both agitated and curious to know what else was in store for them. It was just past 3:20 as Richard Rozario stood up again. They sensed more serious stuff was to follow.

"Ladies and gentlemen, I must thank you for your undivided attention in the pre-tea session. I urge you to think with me in the post-tea session. It will be equally momentous," Richard exhorted them, and continued: "You recall Raphael summarizing for us what he thought defined a professional. Let us put down the points." Then he began writing on the whiteboard.

A professional should be a person:
01. Open.
02. Prepared to continually learn.
03. Able to effectively manage resources.
04. Ready to improve his knowledge.
05. Organized and systematic.
06. Positive, optimistic and friendly.
07. Respectful of people.
08. Free of double standards.
09. Good at Communicating.
10. Exceptional with interpersonal skills.

Looking directly at Raphael he said: "This is fairly comprehensive, Raphael. Do accept my compliments."
"Thank you, Mr. Rozario, you make my day." Raphael returned the compliment.
"Has anyone points to add to the list?" Richard asked.
"Broadly they cover a professional's attitudes, skills, knowledge, and work habits, but I am not sure if the list is complete," Jonathan added.
"The list can never be complete. One can always go on adding points. We are looking at the essentials," Marcela suggested.

"For now, we'll put the list on hold and come back to it. We shall make a small departure to look for names of people who are good professionals. Based on what we have learned so far, can you name a few we should study?" Richard shot off at a tangent.

"Jack Welch," Laxmi suggested.

"Ratan Tata," Jonathan added.

"Definitely, these people are seen as successful professionals, we have much to learn from them," Richard agreed. "Can you think of them as models?" he questioned.

"Yes and no," Manju puzzled. "Yes, in the sense they have much to teach us, no, in the sense that they are far from being perfect. They too stumble and fall."

"Put differently, what we need is a model definitely far above the rest of us," Richard extrapolated.

"Yes, very definitely," Lambert affirmed. All eyes turned to him.

"Let us try and put down the qualities this person should have, focusing on people skills. We already mentioned a professional manages people, not a company. Therefore, we should focus on those qualities to help build relationships," Richard suggested, putting put up the next slide.

	TEAM PERSON
1	Sets criteria for team selection
2	Flat structure, readily accessible to teammates
3	Gives them a goal, a mission, and a focus
4	Continually teaches the team
5	Encourages and motivates the team
6	Defends the team against adversaries
7	Chides them when unavoidable
8	Overrules them when necessary
9	Identifies himself with them
10	Delegates
11	Creates trust and confidence, the team believes in him and accepts him
12	Enjoys their obedience and affection
13	Names and trains a successor

Notes were made, then the next slide came up on the screen.

	PEOPLE PERSON
1	Has empathy for people
2	Is not patronizing or condescending

3	Follows the open-door policy	
4	Sets an example through good conduct	
5	Shuns popularity, only focuses on the task, the mission	
6	Does not wallow in self-pity, in tribulation	
7	Is humble (a tree laden with fruit, bends low)	
8	Readily forgives and does not remind the offender of his wrongdoing	
9	Generous in his praise of others, always ready with compliments	
10	Fair and open, has no favorites and no double standards	
11	Rewards generously	
12	Takes the rough with the smooth, with composure	
13	Can almost read the thoughts of people around him	
14	Takes the initiative in building a relationship, especially with those who are timid	
15	Holds himself accountable and expects accountability from others	
16	Has a vision, which he shares with others	
17	Pursues vision with a zest	
18	Handles conflicts with ease	
19	Looks at the weakness of others with understanding, not accusation	
20	Hopes his people will have faith and confidence in him	

When they had finished, the next came up on the screen.

	SKILLED PERSON
1	Has analytical skills which combine well with imaginative and intuitive thinking
2	Has conceptual and creative skills
3	Has motivating and problem-solving skills
4	Has interpersonal skills to sustain successful transactions
5	Has communication skills of a high order
6	Has planning and organizing skills in good measure
7	Has time management skills that earn him praise
8	Has skills to co-ordinate money, material, and infrastructure
9	Has skills to perform consistently, edifying teams and improving performance

After putting up the three slides, Richard stopped.

He closed his laptop and looked at his audience very intently. They were looking up from their pads, even as they finished making notes, but no one spoke.

"I owe the ladies an explanation: 'He' in our discussions does not exclude a 'she'. There is no gender bias. A lady can be the professional we are discussing. I hope I am clear?" They gave him an understanding smile.

"Should a professional be concerned only with building brands, market penetration, market share, creation of assets, financial ratios, and shareholder returns? Can he perform outside of these parameters?" Richard's searching question, had them looking at each other.

"We are accustomed to thinking of professionals operating under such compulsions. It's difficult to visualize anyone operating outside those parameters," Laxmi said persuasively.

"For example, could a professor, or a teacher, be considered a professional? Would a pastor or a preacher be called one?" Richard demanded.

"Not in our context," Jonathan ventured.

"Why?" Anjali asked, speaking up for the first time.

"Maybe, that is not our mindset," Jonathan replied.

"Since we are on the subject of change, should we not change our mindsets and consider the basic profile of the professional? He is one who effectively manages resources," George argued.

"If we stretch it, 'yes' would be the answer," Jonathan conceded.

"In which case, people like Mahatma Gandhi, Martin Luther King Jr., and Mother Teresa, were professionals?" George persisted.

"In a way, yes," Jonathan agreed.

"Good. So, we are not stuck with people like Jack Welch or Bill Gates or Ratan Tata", Richard concluded.

"No, we can look beyond them," Jonathan generously complied.

"In which case, the list of traits, qualities, we put up for an extraordinary model could serve as a guideline, even if it is not Steve Jobs," Richard was trying hard to connect.

"Someone with those qualities is certainly bigger than Jobs," Marcela stated firmly.

"Could you think of someone who can fit the frame?" Raphael asked.

"Yes." Richard now knew he could not hold out any longer.

They had reached the tipping point of the meeting.

"And who do you have in mind?" Raphael checked.

"**Jesus Christ**," Richard declared.

Jonathan almost jumped off his chair and quickly looked at Raphael, Marcela, Jordan, George and then at Lambert, the other Christians in the room.

Lambert and George were unruffled.

How can these people pick Jesus Christ, Jonathan wondered? But he chose to remain silent.

Latif was not amused. He looked angry.

The others looked around to check reactions.

They were amused at first, assuming that Richard was joking.

Then they turned grim when they found that he was serious.

"Jesus Christ is not a professional. He is a religious leader!" Latif exclaimed.

"He was a religious leader. Why can't he be considered a professional? Didn't he effectively manage his resources?" Richard contended.

"In which case, why not call the prophet of Islam, a model professional?" Latif was incensed.

"You have a point there," Richard affirmed. "He, too, can be a Model-Professional. We have not studied his background. We have studied the background of Jesus."

"So, even Lord Krishna can be treated as a Model-Professional?" Muthukrishnan asked.

"Yes. We are not averse to examining anyone. We chanced to study the life and teachings of Jesus. We found enough reason to put him up as a model," Richard explained.

"But we know little of him," Manju protested.

"Now, you know very little of him. But you can get to know him if you have an open mind. We believe, as professionals, we have open minds," George took up the issue, recalling his own closed responses when Joseph brought it up the first time.

"As professionals, we are supposed to have open minds," Jordan stated matter-of-factly.

"Not supposed to have, but must have," George corrected.

"So, with an open mind, we can look at the life and operations of Jesus. Not in the religious sense and not to agree with our Christian teammates, but to find in Jesus a professional whom we can set up as a model. To help, we have copies of the New Testament for you and additional reading material. Once you have studied it, you will see what we have seen," Richard entreated.

He paused and asked, "Are we agreed on the action?"

They nodded, but not with conviction. They had the odd feeling they were being rushed into this project.

As Richard finished, Joseph walked into the room.

"Good afternoon. How is it going with everyone?" he asked.

"At first, they were confused. Now they are, at least grudgingly, ready to investigate." Richard summed up his conclusions, glancing around the room for confirmation.

Joseph rose and surveyed his team - Good performers, young expectant faces. The future of the company lay in their hands. The company needed them and counted on them. It was important, they understood the idea and accept it, otherwise, no change was possible. His ground-breaking team had to break ground!

"Ladies and gentlemen" he started, "Perhaps you wonder why your counterparts from the other departments aren't here, this afternoon. Especially when you are trying to understand new ideas. You are the ones in direct contact with our customers. You are in touch with the market. Your responses are important, very important. The responses from the other departments will also be important but because you interact with customers, we need your responses first. In the fourth quadrant of the 360-degree Appraisal, the fact that we will seek feedback from customers should explain it. Marketing reaches our customers directly. Without customers, good and loyal customers, there is no company.

Anything we do internally must translate into customer benefits. It is not just about the inputs you give or the output you get, but the impact you make on customers. That is why we chose to speak with you first. We will repeat the exercise with the other divisions." He stopped, took a sip of water, and looked at his audience to pick up signals. There were mixed signals, anticipation in some, apathy in others.

Then he continued, "Mr. Richard Rozario and the other Vice Presidents have tried, in the time available, to put across some ideas to you. These ideas may seem strange, yet they have not been placed before you without forethought. The Vice Presidents and I have done much thinking and debating. Mr. Rozario placed those ideas before you in a capsule form. As pharmaceutical people, you have many capsules in your product range, therefore, you will understand the relevance. This capsule has two colors. The first color represents the 360-degree Appraisal we plan to introduce in stages. We gather General Electric initiated the use of the tool. Some Indian companies are trying to make it compatible with their operations. I've learned, Reliance, Godrej, Wipro, Flipkart, and Infosys are a few of them. When we join this select group, we will be in exalted company. The system is not without its drawbacks. What are those shortcomings?"

"First, there could be bias, positive or negative, of the person doing the rating. Second, the one assessed may sense humiliation and find it difficult to accept negative feedback. Some may even wonder if this exercise is a witch-hunt? Third, there are difficulties and limitations in linking such an appraisal with rewards, such as increments and promotions. Fourth, to ensure the feedback is confidential and fair. In passing, let me add that Flipkart, the fast-growing on-line company, has had problems ensuring their appraisals were fair. When we introduce the system, we plan to make feedback anonymous to prevent negative fall-out from anyone. Fifth, there is a danger that the feedback obtained is not put to good use and totally ignored. What do we have on the merit side? First, the management style of the person is assessed. The methods each uses to achieve results. Some introspection normally follows feedback. Because of the dividends guaranteed for improved performance, s/he may decide to pursue excellence. Second, to change, to improve, and to be accountable, subtle pressure is experienced. Third, with so much feedback given, teamwork will improve. Fourth, it will teach us to delegate. We will understand empowerment. Fifth, this is the true test. Some of our hidden frailties could get exposed. Much to our surprise, some of the skeletons could fall out of the cupboard. Since our intention is to use this tool for improvement, we will put the findings to good use."

"Let me tell you what happened to Mr. Godrej, Chief Executive of Godrej. When the 360-degree Appraisal was introduced in his company, he set an example by being the first to be assessed. To his surprise, he discovered his managers wanted him to be less authoritarian. He perceived himself differently but here were managers telling him he should change. Taking a cue from Mr. Godrej, I propose to be the first in our company to take the 180-degree Appraisal. I will also do it first at the 270-degree stage, and finally the first to do the 360-degree Appraisal. As you get to know the manner in which it is administered, you will find that many of your fears are baseless. We are working on the project. Mr. Rozario hopes to be ready with 180-degree in about 4-6 weeks. Then, we will get back to you."

"You recall I mentioned the capsule has two colors. I said one color represented the 360-degree appraisal system. It is obvious the new appraisal system focuses on relationships. Broadly, our relationships are divided into two types, external and internal. The external relationships are those that we build with people outside the company: Customers, Suppliers, Agents, and others. The internal relationships are built with seniors, peers, juniors and top management. The 360-degree tries to cover the spectrum. If you extend the reasoning, you will find life itself is a network of relationships. The happy man is the one who ensures good relationships with all: family, friends, colleagues and associates. Our success in life depends largely on how we redefine our relationships. Targeting relationships, we tried to find a model for ourselves. A model to help us put relationships in perspective. With the help of the model we need to transform our relationships. Raise our standards and find the impetus to try harder. In short, empower us to become better professionals and human beings.

We discovered Jesus Christ from the Gospels. We discovered him, not by design, but by accident. Recently I chanced to read the Gospels, something I had not done. That is how I got to know more of Jesus. With the little I gained by reading the Gospels, I persuaded the VPs to read them, too. Then, we decided to get more information on Jesus. Afterward, the Vice Presidents and I discussed our findings. We were overwhelmed, none of us wants you to imagine there is a religious angle to this attempt. We only looked at him as a professional. We found outstanding qualities in him and realized there were very few contenders to match him. At least, from those we know, he is the answer to our questions.

Now, we are not against examining other options. People who have stellar qualities like Jesus. It could be an ongoing process. We are open to suggestions. For now, Jesus strikes us as a remarkable model. The other color in the capsule represents Jesus. The 360-degree appraisal is fulfilled in Jesus, the epitome of professional relationships, or the change agent. I do understand that this concept is difficult to grasp; so, you need to do your own reading. You have not met Jesus and made his acquaintance. You now have your opportunity. Mr. Rozario has given you copies of the New Testament and copies of reading material the VP's and I have studied."

"I have a suggestion to offer. You can read the extra sheets and at least the Gospel of Mathew. Then, we can meet on Sunday, before you return to your offices. Is that okay?"
"Let's not disturb their Sunday plans," Lambert pleaded.
"Why not meet on Saturday afternoon?" Richard asked.
"Will they be able to finish reading the material?" Joseph inquired.
"I should think so if they set aside a few hours tonight and a few hours tomorrow," George suggested.
"Well then, at 3:05 tomorrow, we shall meet. I promise you, we shall not keep you beyond two and a half or three hours. If we stay later, it will be because you want to stay on."
Now, the conference was officially over, they wanted to go home.
Joseph added, "We shall say goodnight now. As you leave, please collect from Mr. Rozario copies of two more articles. One is titled, Jesus the unrivaled Communicator. The other is, Leadership and Change. These are in addition to the other articles you have received. After you have made your acquaintance with Jesus, we look forward to seeing you tomorrow."

Chapter Fourteen: Jesus the Unrivaled Communicator

"The person who is eloquent of speech and unafraid of the assembly is hard to defeat in a debate." The Indian Poet, Thiruvalluvar (Verse 647).

The Marketing Managers and Regional Managers were lodged at Taj Coromandel, one of the top hotels in Chennai. After they left the Summit Room, Raphael took the initiative and summoned the rest into his room. "We are going to do our reading now." Despite feeble dissent, they all filed into his room. After they were seated, and slowly savored the hot chocolate he ordered, Manjula began to read from a set of papers.

* * *

One of the many reasons Jesus was special, was that he had strong skills. One of them was his fine-tuned ability to touch the heads and hearts of people, with inspiring thoughts and well-chosen words. Therefore, his powerful communication skills are placed alongside his magnetic personality and charisma. Jesus wrote nothing. He spoke mostly in Aramaic, a Hebrew dialect. So, only his verbal communication is assessed. Strangely, even his silence spoke effectively. The high priests and Pilate, the Governor, discovered his silence was potent.

The Gospels use different words (amazed, astonished, astounded, spellbound) to convey the impact Jesus had on his listeners. Equally convinced, experts over the centuries, have extolled his unmatched communication skills. Certainly, his tools and techniques, and his ability to hold the attention of an audience were the envy of many.

What were those **tools**? How did he deploy them?

1) As a gifted storyteller, Jesus used the Parable as one of the more effective tools (Matt 13:34). Parables are stories of human interest in the social, political and economic context. Farms and farm life, merchants and commerce, noblemen and servants, the temple and devotees, the law and its practice, feasts, and festivals were kernels in his stories. These compact stories with a moral helped preserve the message. Years later, as people reflected on what Jesus taught, his parables came to mind in vivid detail. Some writers refer to these parables as earthly stories with a heavenly intent. The stories he told were simple, direct and very compelling like the Prodigal Son (considered to be the perfect short story), the Lost Sheep, the Lost Coin, and the Good Samaritan. They have not lost their relevance despite many repetitions down the ages.

The timeless parable of the Good Samaritan proves the point that he used such stories to good effect, *"Just then a lawyer stood up to test Jesus. 'Teacher', he said, 'What must I do to inherit eternal life?' He said to him, 'What is written in the law? What do you read there?' He answered, 'You shall love the Lord your God with all your heart and with all your soul and with all your strength and with all your mind, and your neighbor as yourself.' And he said to him, 'you have given the right answer? Do this, and you will live?' Wanting to justify himself, he asked Jesus, 'And who is my neighbor?'*

Jesus replied, 'A man was going down from Jerusalem to Jericho, and fell into the hands of robbers, who stripped him, beat him, and went away, leaving him half dead. Now, by chance, a priest was going down that road; and when he saw him, he passed by on the other side. So likewise, a Levite, when he came to the place and saw him, passed by on the other side. But a Samaritan while traveling came near him; and when he saw him, he was moved with pity. He went to him and bandaged his wounds, having poured oil and wine on them. Then he put him on his own animal, brought him to an inn, and took care of him. The next day he took out two denarii, gave them to the innkeeper, and said, 'Take care of him; and when I come back, I will repay you whatever more you spend.' Which of these three, do you think, was a neighbor to the man who fell into the hands of the robbers?' He said, 'The one who showed mercy.' Jesus said to him, 'Go and do likewise'" Luke 10:25-37.

Notice, in one parable, Jesus juxtaposes the behavior of the priest, the Levite, the bandits, the innkeeper, and the Samaritan. One chooses to care; the others turn away or exploit the traveler. His admonishment, "Go and do likewise" was the right way to end his lesson. Lessons had to be lived, not just heard.

Religious leaders, power brokers, and impostors were constantly trying to stop Jesus with a barrage of tough questions. Jesus' style of handling such tough questions contrasts sharply with Saint Paul. The apostle Paul wrapped concepts in theological words and gave a formal explanation. In careful prose, Paul patiently probed such complex concepts as forgiveness and justification. Jesus, speaking to restless crowds of thousands, communicated the same message in stories. Those stories express the message as well as any scholarly work.

"Has Mr Richard learned from Jesus, on how to tell stories?" Muthu Krishan asked innocently. "Perhaps he has; anyone, can learn from Jesus," Raphael answered.

2) For people to understand what he said, they had to listen. He urged them to do just that (Matt 15:10). Not content with such persuasion, he double-checked if they really understood his words, since he was addressing a cross-section drawn from different backgrounds (Matt 13:51). By following this method, Jesus employed one of the basics in communication, understanding and being understood, through careful listening. If one did not understand, how would one respond? Conscious of the limitations of the listening crowds, Jesus avoided long arguments. Instead, emphasizing the need for people to change their behavior, he adapted his message to their level, never overburdening them (John 16:12).

3) With Jesus, it was not a monologue, a one-way street in the traffic of words. He liked involving his listeners, inviting them to participate, challenging them to put on their thinking caps. He quizzed them (Matt 18:12). And when they had donned their thinking caps, he astounded them with logical arguments and earthy common sense. The passage below illustrates this point, *"No one sews a piece of un-shrunk cloth on an old cloak, for the patch pulls away from the cloak, and a worse tear is made. Neither is new wine put into old wineskins, otherwise, the skins burst, and the wine is spilled, and the skins are destroyed, but new wine is put into fresh wineskins, and so both are preserved"* Matt 9:16-17. He meant the old order had to give way to the new. His listeners understood those situations, which were really their situations, drawn from daily experiences, and readily related to them.

4) What was his attitude to these listeners? He respected their freedom. Compassionately, he proposed but did not impose his thinking on them. For example, a section of his disciples negatively responded to one of his teachings and decided to no longer walk with him (John 6:60). Jesus did not call back those dissenters and dilute his teaching to win their loyalty. On another occasion, when a rich young man walked away from Jesus, unable to respond positively to the option Jesus offered him, of selling all he had to follow him, he did not call him back to negotiate conditions for discipleship.

5) Since his listeners had studied scripture (the Old Testament), to connect with a point he was trying to make, **Jesus often quoted passages from it.** When quoting from scripture, Jesus knew he was on the common ground because many of his listeners had not just read scripture but memorized passages from it. He chose his lines from scripture appropriately. When the Pharisees accused the hungry Apostles of plucking and eating grain on the Sabbath, Jesus quoted what King David had done in the past (Matt 12:3).

By doing so, he was using the proven method of reinforcing the existing beliefs of his listeners.

6) Jesus used clever rejoinders and repartee with telling effect. Those who dared to trap him had to be careful, very careful. Usually, their tactics backfired as Jesus expertly redirected their questions on them. His debating skills were so sharp that his opponents were often impaled on them. Watch this, *"He left that place and entered their synagogue; a man was there with a withered hand, and they asked him, 'Is it lawful to cure on the Sabbath?' so that they might accuse him. He said to them, 'Suppose one of you has only one sheep and it falls into a pit on the Sabbath; will you not lay hold of it and lift it out? How much more valuable is a human being than a sheep! So, it is lawful to do good on the Sabbath.'"* Matt 12:9-12.

7) When some of the Pharisees and Sadducees tried to tease him with awkward questions, the technique of **question for question** worked effectively, as in the following situation: *"Some Pharisees came, and to test him they asked, 'Is it lawful for a man to divorce his wife?' He answered them, 'What did Moses command you?'"* Mark 10:2-3. When he had their answer to his question, he chose to answer. At other times, when he knew that the question was genuine, and not intended to test him, he chose to answer the question readily. In the parable of the Good Samaritan, we find that the opening remarks are an example of his question-for-question technique.

Laxmi signaled Manjula, that she would take over. With remarkable zeal, she started.

8) Whether he spoke with his disciples or the crowd, **Jesus was the epitome of courtesy** (Luke 7:40). And his idea of courtesy included slipping in a lesson on etiquette at the table. *"When he noticed how the guests chose the places of honor, he told them a parable. 'When you are invited by someone to a wedding banquet, do not sit down at the place of honor, in case someone more distinguished than you has been invited by your host; and ,the host who invited both of you may come and say to you, 'give this person your place', and then in disgrace you would start to take the lowest place. But when you are invited, go and sit down at the lowest place, so that when your host comes, he may say to you, "Friend, move up higher'; then you will be honored in the presence of all who sit at the table with you'."* Luke 14:7-10. Discern his skill in communicating the lesson. He stressed on the benefit, the advantage, the honor the person would get by following his suggestion. To motivate someone to do something, show him how he will benefit.

It's a tip, good communicators offer us. Jesus used the method with distinction, much before experts gave us such advice.

9) His communication was always relevant – to his audience, and to the occasion. In Luke 15 the Pharisees and Scribes complain that Jesus kept the company of sinners. He replies to them by narrating three parables: The Lost Sheep (3-7), The Lost Coin (8-10) and The Lost Son, known as the Prodigal Son (11-32). Notice he addresses the difficulty his listeners have in reconciling the presence of a holy person in the midst of wrong doers. How can a Rabbi, like him, befriend sinners? Using the parables, he explains why he is compassionate to sinners. He will not join them in wrongdoing, but gently and patiently lead them from vice to virtue. The crowds listening to him are drawn from a mix of shepherds, flock-owners, fathers and mothers and all who have a lasting interest in money. That is why they have no problem relating to his message, as he uses their situations and their idiom, sheep, money, and children. Eloquently, to teach his lesson, he blends the context with the message. The fit is perfect. Going after the lost is his purpose, redeeming the sinner is his priority. He concludes, reconciling the wrong doer with God is a responsibility no one can shirk.

10) Look carefully at the audiences Jesus addresses. Is he talking to one person, his disciples, a crowd, or his opponents? He treats each differently. It seemed he took words, scrubbed them clean, washed them in running water and laid them before his listeners. They sparkled. The sparkle came from the figures of speech he used with practiced ease. *"I have said these things to you in figures of speech"* John 16:25. There was a liberal use of vivid similes in his speech. In Matt 10:16 we have an example: *"See, I am sending you like sheep into the midst of wolves; so be wise as serpents and innocent as doves."*

Sustained metaphors punctuated his speech. Describing his followers as the salt and light of the earth, Jesus said: *"You are the salt of the earth; but if salt has lost its taste, how can its saltiness be restored? It is no longer good for anything but is thrown out and trampled underfoot. You are the light of the world. A city built on a hill cannot be hidden. No one after lighting a lamp puts it under the bushel basket, but on the lampstand and it gives light to all in the house. In the same way, let your light shine before others"* Matt 5:13-16. Metaphorically, he identified himself as the true vine (John 15:1), and the Good Shepherd (John 10:11). Speaking to his Apostles, he compared their mission to fishing (Mathew 4:19) and harvesting (Mathew 9:37). Occasionally, he used the hyperbole with a stunning effect. The following verse is an example: *"Again I tell you, it is easier for a camel to go through the eye of a needle than for someone who is rich to enter the kingdom of God"* Matt 19:24. With the hyperbole, the statement is difficult to understand. Minus the hyperbole, Jesus was suggesting that we should not get obsessed with or attached to money. He selectively used the epigram: *"The greatest among you will be your servant"* Matt 23:11. And the Paradox had his listeners wondering: *"For those who want to save their life will lose it, and those who lose their life for my sake will find it"* Matt 16:25. He loved ironies and little riddles: *"But many who are first will be last, and the last will be first"* Matt 19:30. And in Matt 7: 9-10, he referred to a father who would not give his son a stone when the boy asked for bread, or give him a serpent when he wanted a fish. His deft play of words was not lost on listeners when he said: *"You blind guides! You strain out a gnat (Aramaic - galma) but swallow a camel (Aramaic-gamla)"* Matt 23: 24. Sparing use of rhetoric gave his statements a rare verve: *"Are grapes gathered from thorns or figs from thistles?"* Matt 7:16

11) How would one describe the imagery he brought to his speech? *"Consider the lilies, how they grow: they neither toil nor spin; yet I tell you, even Solomon in all his glory was not clothed like one of these."* Luke 12:27

12) Jesus spiced his talks with axioms, dictums, and expressions that were seemingly trite. *"For where your treasure is, there your heart will be also"* Luke 12:34. And, *"Can a blind person guide a blind person?"* Luke 6:39 and *"One sows, and another reaps"* John 4:37. Pithy, power-packed punch lines (the alliteration is intended).

13) In the three years of his public ministry, **Jesus was constantly answering questions** raised by friends and foes. In the process, his list of questions was not shortened: *"But who do you say I am?"* Matt 16:15; and, *"Do you want to be made well?"* John 5:6.

14) Jesus was serious in his communication; never flippant. But there were times when his listeners could not help smiling when they caught the funny tilt. *"Why do you see the speck in your neighbor's eye, but do not notice the log in your own eye? Or, how can you say to your neighbor, 'Let me take the speck out of your eye' while the log is in your own eye?"* Matt 7:3-4

15) Sometimes, Jesus used the very situation, the context in which they were, to give his listeners a message: *"He sat down opposite the treasury, and watched the crowd putting money into the treasury.*

Many rich people put in large sums. A poor widow came and put in two small copper coins, which are worth a penny. Then he called his disciples and said to them, 'Truly I tell you, this poor widow has put in more than all those who are contributing to the treasury, for all of them have contributed out of their abundance. But she out of her poverty has put in everything she had, all she had to live on'" Mark 12:41-44.

16) Jesus did not compromise on his teaching. His listeners knew he was uniquely consistent in his thought process. Pope John Paul II was emphatic on how Jesus' words and deeds were 'never separable' from his life. His convictions were deep-rooted and strong. His words conveyed those convictions and his actions were consistent with his words. Everything tied up, without a contradiction. He was singularly unique.

Jesus had several titles conferred on him. The most commonly used was the teacher. In his role as a teacher, his communication skills found full play. He was known to use the precise diction of a teacher, which combined remarkably with his limitless patience in reaching out to those he was teaching. Like his versatile personality, his communication had variety and class, simplicity and profound meaning, pin-pointed appeal, and unrelenting persuasive power. Just like the drop that hollows the stone not by force, but by falling often, Jesus persuaded his listeners gently. As a good communicator, he knew his audience (drawn from different castes, classes, regions, professions, political systems), and adapted to their needs, and they responded to him.

Once again, what are the words in the Gospels that describe his impact on listeners: **Amazed, Astonished, Astounded, Spellbound.**

* * *

There was silence in the room, each caught up in intriguing thoughts, until Latif ventured an opinion. "Is Marcela able to get the better of us because of her communication skills?"
Marcela chuckled. "Yes. She is also smart," Muthu Krishnan suggested.
"Well then, let her be our spokesperson in the session tomorrow," Jordan urged.
Marcela protested. "No. Each of us will have our thoughts to share. Each one speaks for himself or herself." Raphael agreed with her.

Chapter fifteen: Leadership and change

"Change is not merely necessary to life. It is life." Alvin Toffler.

Lambert drove straight from the meeting to the office of Frank Morris, a leadership consultant, and his classmate in business school. Frank was waiting for Lambert, who gave him Joseph's sheets on leadership, the ninth in the series. Lambert had spoken to Frank on the article and wanted his opinion. Frank decided to take some time out to help his friend. After a few casual comments, Frank began to read the article.

* * *

Only leaders who walk tall can initiate and sustain change. Those who cannot walk tall, trip and fall. Leaders who are dwarfed by the compromises they make cannot fill the huge footprints of leaders who walk tall. They step into one print but cannot reach the next. For them the struggle is unending. Although they know the values and virtues of the highways, they choose the lures and vices of the byways. Caught in a tangle of their own making, they cry for relief and release, but both are slow to come to them. Therefore, it is right we return to the basics, to understand how the tall leader's plan works.

In simple terms, management is coping with complexity, and leadership is initiating and coping with change. A professional should manage both. When he effectively manages his resources, he is handling complex situations. Built into those complex situations are changes he must usher in speedily and decisively, despite the popular vote against them. At times he is alone, trusting the change he is trying to bring about will prompt his teammates to support him. Sometimes, even that solace is not his. Yet, he must move on, to put into action what he believes. Peter Drucker, the peerless management guru, believed that leadership and management are inseparable, they fuse for producing results. This is why his concept of management was known as the practical way to quantifiable outcomes.

A complete agreement does not exist on what exactly constitutes the job of a professional. Different researchers and writers have tried to examine his functions and put down their thoughts. A satisfactory, homogenous description is difficult to find. One thing is clear though, the professional must cope with complexities from the very act of effectively managing resources. Some writers give importance to the profit maximization objective. They say the professional must strive for profits, at all costs. He owes it to the shareholders. Others believe there is more to it than just money. They believe that a value-driven professional can set the tone, in an organization, for a value-system, and that the profits will follow. Almost like suggesting to a marketing manager to focus on customer satisfaction and customer delight. Once he does that, he need have no worry because profits will follow.

In a thought-provoking conversation with the Editor in Chief, Adi Ignatius, of Harvard Business Review (March – April 2018), Kenneth Frazier, CEO of Merck Pharmaceuticals made some remarkable assertions, *"I think businesses also exist to deliver value to society."* Not content, he affirms, *"The revenue and shareholder value are an imperfect proxy for the value we create for patients and society."* And, he stressed, *"If you are just focused on trying to make money, you are not going to be successful in the long run."* To sum up he added: *"It is critical to know where you stand."* To prove his point, he was the first to resign from President Trump's American Manufacturing Council; then the world knew where he stood. The compromises and consequences in the cases of Volkswagen (exposed for systemic deception on emission levels of its vehicles), Wells Fargo (fraudulent accounts), and Petrobras, Brazil, (widespread bribery), only lend strength to Frazier's case that making money at all costs has its hidden perils; the alchemy of base objectives to refined ideals does not work. Earlier, on April 24, 2010, The Economist reported that Paul Polman, boss of Unilever, told the Financial Times: *"I do not work for the Shareholder, to be honest; I work for the consumer, the customer---. I am not driven, and I do not drive this business model by driving Shareholder value."* More and more CEOs now endorse maximizing customer satisfaction or Customer-driven Capitalism. Some names and their statements follow. Jim Treybig, of Tandom, said every person is a human being and deserves to be treated as one. The late J.R.D. Tata had a similar point to make. Kenneth Blanchard emphatically writes, *"There is nothing so unequal, as the equal treatment of unequals."* Cooper Procter of Procter and Gamble ran the company with the slogan: *"Do what is right."* Theodore Vail of AT & T stressed superior customer service. Robert Townsend wrote: *"If you have a policy manual, publish the Ten Commandments."* Such stars brightened the path they chose, shedding light for their teams, as well.

To set a direction, leaders must have a clear mission. What is mission? It is the turbo-charged engine that drives leadership. It powers the leader to anticipate and plan. It means foresight and direction, getting others to share the mission, and inspiring them to follow. Without mission the leader and the Institution are dead.

To actualize his mission, the leader must take decisions. Decision-making becomes an important activity, as Lou Pritchett stressed in *Stop Paddling and start rocking the boat*, *"One trait of the true leader is decisiveness; if you can't make a decision you probably aren't cut out to be a leader."* In making decisions, a leader can come face to face with paradoxes, which he must resolve. Jack Welch has a point to make, *"Effective leadership involves the acceptance and management of a paradox."* In effect, he is making two points. First, accept the paradoxical situation. Don't resent it, you have to live with it. Second, plan to manage the situation.

The leader must see every problem, even a paradox, as an opportunity which will take him closer to actualizing his mission. Alan Stoneman, former President of Purex Corporation said, *"We have no problems here, all are opportunities."* Mother Teresa had something similar to say. She said a difficulty, or a problem was not a curse but a blessing. Put differently, she was trying to tell us that the way we see the problem, is the problem. Almost identical thoughts were paraphrased by Stephen R Covey when he explained that effective people are not problem oriented. They are opportunity-driven, they feed the opportunity and starve the problem. In his problem solving, or opportunity-feeding attempts, the leader must build trust. Otherwise, his attempts to problem-solve will fail.

Successful leaders are known to have traits identified by Henry Mintzberg. These traits include brevity, variety, action-orientation, strong oral communication. Such traits lend them some dynamism. You spot them readily. They are the Achievers. These achievers are flexible, not bound by tradition, and not shackled by obdurate mindsets.

How does Jesus fit into such a framework? Take his mission, in the three years of his public ministry. His mission was set, and he pursued it unfailingly. He communicated his mission to his team and motivated them enough to make his purpose their own. In later years his disciples lived and died in defense of his mission. In arriving at decisions, he was decisive, not wavering. Whether he was selecting a team or empowering them or challenging the system or confronting the hypocrites or choosing locations to visit or synagogues to go in and teach, he did not hesitate. Even if the decision was tough; even when a paradox had to be resolved.

Look at the number of times he converted a problem into a teaching-opportunity. The adulteress is brought to him, so he may condemn her. Her accusers think he has no way out. Yet she is acquitted, not just because he forgives her, but because he turns the law back on them.

Should the tax be paid to Caesar? A 'yes' would mean the rebels who wanted freedom from Rome would see him as a stooge of Rome. A 'no' would mean that he was going against Caesar. Give to Caesar what belongs to Caesar and to God what belongs to him, he answers. He used each situation not just to silence his opponents but, chiefly to teach all his listeners a lesson.

We find many occasions in the Gospels when people place their faith in him; they trusted him. His disciples trusted him because he was open and fair and honest. There was no dichotomy between his words and deeds, he preached forgiveness and readily forgave even his sworn enemies, because he genuinely respected and loved people. He showed that a true leader needed no props and no crutches.

His personality, not given to judging others, attracted both the ordinary folk and the open-minded upper classes. His teachings and debates were brief and to the point, nudging people into action. His skill in verbal communication was so outstanding that Thomas Jefferson referred to it as *'the sublime eloquence'*. People wondered at the ease with which he debated with the Doctors of Law and demolished their arguments. The variety of subjects he handled astounded even the elders.

He was an action-oriented leader, not laid back or given to passive responses. For him each moment was important. Each day was one day less in his 3-year ministry. Much was to be done and he could not wait or relax. We have plenty of proof of his situational management skills in the Gospels.

Carefully examine the different methods he uses to tutor Peter. Watch the different styles he uses to contend with the opposition. He was constantly adapting to the situation. He did not get stale or predictable, because he was continually finding new ways of doing things and coming up with situation-specific solutions.

Employing such a formidable combination of qualities, he brought about far-reaching changes. He toppled established practices, including the strict observances of the Sabbath. Totally unafraid, he challenged the archaic system, proposing a non-violent method of resolving disputes, strongly recommending forgiveness instead of retaliation, and daring his listeners to try out a new way of life - the love of God and love of neighbor. He was different even in choosing his disciples. At that time, the practice was that a disciple chose a rabbi and followed him. Jesus broke with convention when he chose disciples.

As a true leader, he offered his followers something to believe in and a direction to take to actualize that belief. He showed them the means and methods to face challenges when pursuing their mission.

What do we notice when a strong wind has passed? A lot of things are out of place. So was society when Jesus passed their way. Beliefs were questioned. Many practices seemed meaningless. A new order was in the making because a new kind of professional, a new kind of leader, was at work.

* * *

Lambert did not stop Frank as he read. When the reading was over, Lambert asked: "Are you saying you endorse it?" Lambert probed.

"Undoubtedly" Frank asserted and asked: "Would you mind if I keep this copy?"

"Yes." Lambert responded, "I have another copy."

The two lapsed into silence until Lambert reminded Frank, he had to meet Richard the same evening. They shook hands and Lambert drove out of the driveway.

Chapter Sixteen: A Formidable Combination

"A good head and a good heart are always a formidable combination." Nelson Mandela.

After the disturbing session on Friday, the group was more relaxed and expectant today. A day in between had given them time to think. Reading the material they were given, they were better equipped to ask questions and provide answers. They also knew what was coming. It was 3:05 pm on Saturday, as they reassembled to attend to unfinished business.

Richard Rozario rose and spoke with his customary courtesy, "Ladies and gentlemen, thank you for coming on a Saturday afternoon and coming on time. I take it you have read the material you collected yesterday and feel richer by the experience."

Latif Basha, who had raised objections on Friday, seemed anxious to speak: "Mr. Rozario besides reading the extra material you gave me, I found the time to read Mathew."
"You have given today's meeting a good start," Richard commended him.
"In the additional material you gave us, the passages from the Bible stand out; there is only sparse commentary. The passages speak for themselves," Laxmi inferred.
"Like pearls strung together, they glitter." Jonathan's simile gave Laxmi's comment some brilliance.
"Laxmi and Jonathan, thank you for your helpful deductions." Richard, who was conscious much had to be done with about three hours to do them, was quick to respond and continued, "Yesterday, we discussed the 360-degree appraisal. We also discussed the attitudes, skills, habits and knowledge attributes of a model, and we set you thinking on Jesus. For a while, let us look at four factors and apply them to Jesus. What can we put down as the attitudes, skills, habits, and knowledge of Jesus?"
"He was honest and fair," Latif declared.
"He was positive and open," Manju added.
"He was courageous and outspoken," Jordan stated.
"May I put down those points under the head of attitudes?" Richard asked.
"Yes," Jonathan agreed. Richard then wrote down the points on the whiteboard and turning to his audience and asked, "What more?"
"Towards wealth and money, he had a detached attitude," Marcela added.

"I think he was a people-person. Like a magnet attracting iron filings, he attracted people," Muthukrishnan gushed.

"I think he was consistent in what he said and did, there was no double-speak," Marcela made another point.

"He comes across as a very committed person. He had a mission and was wedded to it," Jonathan said and added, "A self-effacing incident comes to mind. Jesus has been with the crowds for the whole day working wondrous deeds for them. An eventful day comes to a close. Early the next day he goes out and the disciples look for him. After much searching, they find him and tell him of the huge impact he has had on the people. Even now, they say, people are looking for him everywhere. Instead of going to them to be congratulated and praised, he tells his apostles they will leave immediately for other places where they will have to spread the Good News. Unlike most of us, who would go after applause and distraction, he stayed focused on his mission."

"Thank you. Jonathan, you made an important point. We have put down these points under his attitude. Let us now move to his skills." Richard was polite, yet firm.

"He was a great communicator; an excellent debater. I do not know of anyone who can match his communication skills," Jordan offered his opinion.

"His skill in resolving conflicts, in handling difficult situations deftly, is something we can all learn from," Laxmi commented.

"His situational management skills were extraordinary - with individuals, his disciples, the crowds, or his tormentors. Remarkable!" Jonathan observed.

"What a storyteller he was! So creative, his stories were beautifully crafted," Raphael remarked.

"Shall we now take up his habits? The idea is to get to the essentials, the important points. We are not planning to make an exhaustive list," Richard explained.

"Jesus was the hands-on type, upfront, saying things, doing things and giving the lead," Laxmi's opinion was well received.

"He was very hard working; always on the move. But he carefully planned breaks for his disciples from the punishing schedule he followed, it was thoughtful of him." Jordan certainly enjoyed the occasional breaks he took.

"Self-disciplined and time conscious, he did not indulge in a wasteful effort," Latif was speaking again.

"Jesus was earnest about setting the right example. Besides the unmatched example he set from the cross, he gave us an enduring example when he washed the feet of his apostles. I cannot think of any CEO washing the feet of his team," Jonathan showed he had reflected on the Gospels.

"Jonathan, you are right. Jesus inspires through the examples he sets in many ways. I only hope we can follow some of his sterling qualities. Now, shall we move on to his knowledge?" Richard said.

"The Gospels do not say how he acquired so much knowledge. But he knew the scriptures well enough to challenge the Doctors of the Law. He could relate to business, legal matters, customs, nature, and so many more subjects. At that time, he could have been called a walking encyclopaedia. Remember, the people were spellbound when he spoke," Raphael had read all the four Gospels more than once, but he made no mention of it.

"Let us try and wrap up this part of our discussion, shall we? We have all the points you listed. The list is impressive. My question to you, do you find something wanting? Could Jesus have done something, he did not do? Was there any gap, which he should have bridged?" Richard cautiously worded his question.

"Yes, I think he should have spoken up during his trial and crucifixion. He let them take advantage of him. He could have silenced them as he silenced others in the past. Even Pilate was just waiting for some signal from him to set him free but, he was silent." Latif was anguished.

"And I think he should have gotten one of his disciples to document all he said and did. We have the Gospels but, chances are, we have missed a lot because it was not written at the time of the event." Jonathan spoke as though it was a personal loss.

"Let us take your two points. First, you say he should have spoken up at his trial. Think of it, his adversaries were fixated on crucifying him. They were in no mood to listen to him. Jesus knew it would serve no purpose if he tried to explain matters. He chose not to speak. In fact, his silence amazed them. They wondered at the strength of his character. Second, you say he should have got someone to record all he said and did. He could have but he was not keen to record his actions. He even discouraged people from speaking of the miracles he performed. What he wanted was for people to reflect on what he said and change.

Come to think of it, even if he wanted them to record his words and deeds, who among his apostles were equipped to record it, perhaps Mathew? Mathew did give us a fairly exhaustive account. John's Gospel was born of great reflection, it could not have been written without reflection. It had to wait. John states at the end of his Gospel that there was much more to be recorded. Why he, who was with Jesus through the three years, did not write more will remain unanswered.

Mark and Luke were not among his disciples, so, recording events into a diary when Jesus was with them did not fit into the scheme of things." The homework Richard had done was evident. "Anything else?" he checked.

"Nothing we can think of, Jesus is a towering personality. We are not equal to the task of picking holes in his life and works," Raphael confessed.

"What comes across from the points you made is that Jesus was a man ahead of his times, committed to a lofty Mission. He was prepared to work very hard to make it happen. He was competent and wise. He was a people-person, ready to help anyone in need. He brought about changes through his teachings, powerfully communicated, and through his exemplary conduct. He was genuine." the agreement with Richard was unanimous.

"Mr. Lambert Kurien, your turn," Richard said as he went back to his seat.

Lambert stood up, he looked impressive in his steel-grey Armani suit. The button-down Louis Philippe white shirt was without blemish. The maroon Van Heusen tie with black spots stood out against his dark jacket. The cuff links he wore glinted in the bright lights of the conference room. All eyes were riveted on him.

"You are marketing professionals who should understand the connection I will try to establish. Someone wisely said, *'Enter through their door to exit through yours.'* I am trying to explain it so that you get the message, admitting it through your window. Jesus was a marketing man, a customer-oriented Professional. Take the variables in marketing. You have a company, marketing products to customers, in conditions, both favorable and unfavorable, having to contend with fierce competition. What have I said? I said there are 4 variables involved, the company, the customer, the conditions, and the competition. They are the 4C's of marketing. Now take the marketing mix. You have a product, sold at a price, through a distribution network, with the help of the right promotion. It means we have 4 more variables, Product, Price, Place, and Promotion, the 4Ps of marketing. In all, there are 8 variables. I said Jesus was a marketing man. Let us see how he managed these variables.

What was his company? Call it, if you like, Jesus Christ Inc., small; no equity, yet full of enthusiasm and zeal, mission propelled. In three years, they were operating in different parts of Palestine. No corporate office. No stationery. Perhaps it was the first paperless office. No computers. No cell phones. No banks to fund projects. They had ambitious plans of going international but were down to earth in handling day-to-day situations. No targets or budgets, only strategies for market situations."

"Who were his customers? Farmers and fisherman, the sick and infirm, the poor and the rich, the famous and the notorious made up the wide spectrum of customers he served. No one was excluded. A large mass market, if you get what I mean. Did he segment his market? In a way he did. He responded readily to the needy. That segment seemed to be his target audience. He was prepared to transact with everyone, The Roman Centurion, Nicodemus (the influential Pharisee) and Zacchaeus, the Chief Tax Collector; anybody."

"What were the conditions in which he operated? The Jews were a subjugated lot. Rome ruled with an iron hand. The Jews were, therefore, an oppressed people, who had to find hope in something. Hope in the liberator, the savior, who was to come and free them from the oppressor, sustained them. A sword-wielding and lance-thrusting fighting hero would liberate them, they believed. The Messiah who appeared, Jesus, was the opposite. They felt let down. A good bit of their resentment toward him was born of their disappointment. They were suspicious of everything he said and everything he did or tried to do, for them, mostly because he did not fit the picture that they painted of the Messiah.

Therefore, their response was tardy; not from the ordinary people but, from the upper classes. The conditions, to say the least, were not favorable. Jesus probably made things worse for himself by exposing the hypocrisy of the opposition. They were bent on stopping his advancement. In such circumstances, what did Jesus have to offer? What was his product? He offered his customers a concept. He was into concept marketing where there was nothing to touch, feel or smell, only an idea, a very different idea. Different from the one the Jews had been taught, beyond the law. The very newness was startling.

"What really was the product? Love, love God, love yourself and love your neighbor. The product was so advanced that people could not comprehend it. The dimensions were difficult to measure. When 'an eye for an eye' was the way of life, how could love and forgiveness fit? When intrigue, hate, and vengeance were commonly traded in, how could his product be bartered? Yet, Jesus was all set to give his product an edge through personal example. He would not rest until the market gave his product a fair chance."

"What was the price he expected for his product? No money. No goods in exchange. No deferred payment. No credit card payment. What he asked for was only faith. Would they want to believe in him? Would they choose to trust him? It was all he wanted."

"Did he incur marketing costs? Very little cost because they traveled on foot and sometimes in a boat. He threw no parties to entertain clients. His hospitality was the sharing of his meager rations. He sent no greeting cards at festival time and had no communication costs. His small needs were met by people who began to share his beliefs, a fraternity that was growing by the day."

"What did he do about a distribution network? He had no distributors and no retailers. Instead, he and his team delivered the product directly to his customers. Jesus led from up-front, meeting his customers and delivering the product to them, literally on a one-to-one basis. Although he addressed groups, he was concerned about each person in the group. He spotted their needs and transacted with them not for a single sale, but for building a relationship. He knew if the trust was built, relationships would peak, and transactions would repeat.

He was into relationship marketing. He had no insurance cover and no claims to be settled. No transit-time restrictions. The delivery system he devised was so successful his customers came to him in droves to do repeat business with him. As he expanded his team from 12 to 82, the new team fellows joined in the supply chain management, although logistics management was centrally monitored. Some of his customers accepted his product with less understanding but, most with nothing short of awe."

"What about promotion? Advertising, the way we know it now, was not in vogue. He communicated his message directly and in simple terms. He got to the head and heart of his listener and to the heart of the subject.

"What techniques did he use? He used parables or stories and examples drawn from family and work life. He spoke their lingo, their idiom. Most understood. And how did the message spread? Not through billboards, posters or handbills. The message spread only through word-of-mouth testimony. Those who came to hear him told others. More came. They too heard him and told still more. The numbers swelled. Testimony, as we know, is a powerful medium, and promotion, not in our mundane sense, was at work."

"How did he position himself? He occupied a position easily identified because it was different. He took a position opposed by popular perception. The law promoted retaliation. Jesus entreated his listeners to forgive their enemies, love those who offended them. He swung the pendulum to the other extreme. His customers could not but notice and they were astounded."

"And what about the additional 4 Ps? What we refer to as People, Pace, Processes, and Packaging. There is universal admission Jesus was a people person, all the time building new bonds, mending broken bonds and building relationships. His pace was hectic, constantly on the move to new places. Alert to any situation, he was half a step ahead of the opposition. He started when he was 30. When we look back at what he accomplished in three years, we are amazed. At 33 he was dead. What were the processes involved? Whether delegating or instructing, healing the sick or feeding the poor, planning a trip to a distant location or visiting a synagogue for a discourse, all processes were simple, linked, and effective. There was no waste of time. No duplication of effort. No waste of any resource."

"How did he package his product? Not in polyethylene or cans, but in easily understood words. His stories were retold thousands of times down the centuries. In vivid examples. He packaged the product keeping his customer in mind, the way the customer would understand and accept the product."

"Through 2000 years, more and more people are beginning to make sense of the very simple concept (product) he promoted because he combined head and heart in appealing to them. He used reason and emotion to touch their heads and hearts. As we do in marketing, Jesus looked at the situation from the customer's point of view."

"So, you see, Ladies and Gentlemen, Jesus was a marketing man, well into concept marketing and into relationship marketing. He was a specialist in CRM (customer relationship marketing). He tried to go beyond customer satisfaction to achieve customer delight and he achieved it with distinction. A popular expression among marketing people is, *'You are confined by the walls you build'*. Jesus broke free of such confinement. I have seen it. You too will see it now." He paused, looked at his audience once more and said, "I thank you for your time and attention," and sat down. Not a word was spoken. Perhaps some wanted to applaud. But none did, everyone was stunned.

It was now Joseph's turn. He looked animated and ready to go but when he found the smokers in the room fidgety, he suggested a ten-minute break.

Chapter Seventeen: Doing the Right Thing

"It is more important to do the right thing than to do things right." Peter Drucker.

As they reassembled, Joseph lost no time in getting started. "Ladies and gentlemen, to points made by Mr. Rozario and Mr. Kurien, let me add a few."

"Jesus sought the transformation of human relations which, in simple terms, means motivating the individual to perform, by recognizing his efforts, encouraging his performance and rewarding him suitably. Combining the human resources and human relations approaches, he spoke of the kingdom of God, not as something distant and unattainable, but as a very real brotherhood of mankind. A place where people could live in peace, with steadfast faith, joyous hope, and untiring love. He believed each person was capable of much. Each had the potential to be realized. Spot that talent; develop it; allow it blossom, was how he saw it. The transformation of Mathew from a tax collector to a loyal disciple is a case in point. The words of Scott Peck come to mind, *'All human interactions are opportunities either to learn or to teach.'* Jesus taught and Mathew learned. Jesus spoke to the crowds and they listened, which was a step in the learning process. I have a slide here, which illustrates a very important point."

After the group had made notes from the slide, Joseph continued, "Trust in a person is the highest tribute you can pay him or her. When people believed in him, when his disciples trusted him, Jesus received a compliment we professionals crave for. Few of us gain it in a

Jesus -the People Person

Builds relationships using the right attitudes, skills, habits and knowledge with..

| Seniors | Peers | Team | Customers |

Resulting in Trust

professional lifetime. Many of us retire and fade, before tasting of its sweetness."

"Yesterday, Mr. Rozario, spoke to you on the 360-degree appraisal. He said it is an effective tool to measure the kind of relationships we build with different segments of people. After spending many hours discussing the new system, the Vice Presidents and I attempted a 360-degree appraisal of Jesus. Mr. Rozario has worked on our comments and prepared a summary highlighting a few essential points. No appraisal for a person like Jesus can be complete." So saying, Victor put up the summary. With the slide up, he paused for a long time. They had taken notes but kept looking at the slide, wanting to know more about Jesus.

Joseph began slowly, "Ladies and gentlemen, this is an intriguing part of my presentation. By now you are familiar with the four quadrants in the 360-degree appraisal. The illustration in this slide is less important. It is just a rough representation of the four segments. The points in it are significant. May I have your undivided attention as I take you through the points in the four quadrants? We had to work with a limitation. We could not interact directly with the different sources for the appraisal, seniors, peers, teammates, and customers of Jesus. We could not administer questionnaires to them. Instead, we had to depend on what we found in the Gospels and make inferences. From the pages of history, those people spoke to us and helped us form opinions."

"In the first 90-degree quadrant, we refer only to seniors, how seniors viewed Jesus. In the second 180-degree quadrant, only responses from peers, the new variable, find a place. In fact, it should hold information on both seniors and peers. To avoid repetition and clutter, we have focused on peers. Likewise, in the third 270-degree quadrant, a relationship with his team is appraised, subordinates, if you please. We have not repeated information from the first and second quadrants. Finally, in the fourth 360-degree quadrant, we focus on his Customers. In effect, the 360-degree appraisal is the sum total of what appears in the four quadrants. Is that clear?" It was clear to them.

"In each quadrant, we record our overall assessment of Jesus for the corresponding variable. We have Very Good for the first and Excellent for the second, third and fourth. Then we explain why we gave Jesus those overall assessments. Yesterday, Mr. Rozario gave you a fairly long list of Jesus' attributes as a people-person, team-person and so on. In the summary you are reading now, we have not reproduced all those points. We have picked a few."

"In the first quadrant, we give Pilate the status of a superior. Not his immediate superior, but as the Roman Governor, he exercised rights over people in the region. Jesus belonged to the region; therefore, the connection. Pilate respected Jesus and was amazed at his regal ways and he tried three times to release him. In fact, he found no fault in him but decreed the crucifixion more out of fear of Rome. Anyone setting himself up as king challenged Caesar's throne. Jesus did not, but the high priests portrayed him as a usurper. The high priests were not Jesus' superiors. In the structure of the time, a Rabbi was at least a level lower than the high priests and Jesus was a Rabbi. It explains our giving some weight to their opinion of Jesus. We all know their opinions were prejudiced. They feared his growing influence and the prospect of being side-lined, they manipulated the crowds to scream for Jesus' death. To contain the threat Jesus supposedly posed, they engineered his downfall by getting him crucified. Despite their villainous ways, they unwittingly and grudgingly paid him a compliment when they keenly and closely followed his actions and words and the impact they had on people. The overall weight we have given the first quadrant is, Very Good. We must remember, in the conventional sense, Jesus did not have a superior. Therefore, the rating given to him in the first quadrant need not carry much weight. The ratings in the other three quadrants are more important. Mr. Rozario, when he has finished his investigations will teach us how to do a proper grading. Until then we shall settle for what we have now done."

"The feedback from Peers appears in the second quadrant. If one were to look at Nicodemus, Zacchaeus, and some others as his peers, it is obvious they occupied fairly high positions and were definitely socially and professionally above his disciples. These peers of Jesus listened to him, were edified by his example and followed his advice. Nicodemus even stood up for Jesus against the Council, jeopardizing his position among the Council members. Zacchaeus showed how seriously he took Jesus' example when he chose to give up his money-grabbing ways. Let us not be misled by some of these peers who were afraid to own up peerage or any association with Jesus. They preferred to seek his counsel late into the night to escape prying eyes. In no way does it detract from the rating Jesus enjoys, it should be a strike against his peers. Therefore, our overall assessment is, Excellent."

"The third quadrant is about the team. How did they respond to him? What had they to say? The reading material we gave you has many points on his relationship with the disciples. He gave them a Mission, and with them, pursued it relentlessly. He trained them and delegated powers to them. He loved them and protected them. Without reserve they obeyed him, and importantly, trusted him, giving up all that they called their own. What more can one expect? The assessment is, Excellent."

"In the fourth quadrant, we have feedback from his customers. What was his message to them? Love. Right through the three years of his public ministry, he found different ways of putting this message across to them. He praised them and motivated them. He helped them and empathized with them. For example, he showed them that all his teachings can be practiced. Almost in return for all that he did for them, they followed him in increasing numbers, and many believed in him. Our overall assessment is: Excellent."

"Now, you know if more factors were put into it, we would have a more detailed illustration and a distinctly better rating; our inference is drawn from a sample. Our sample speaks to us of the whole. In this appraisal, we cannot ignore the cowardly behavior of the disciples at the time of Jesus' arrest and crucifixion. We should try to understand why they behaved in the way they did. Their devotion to him was never in doubt, but fear of arrest, torture, and death, made them flee. Like normal humans who put distance between themselves and danger, the disciples took flight.

"We also witness the rabid behavior of his customers, the common people, during the crucifixion. How do we explain that? Two points strike me: One, the common folk obeyed their priests and elders; such obedience was built into their psyche. These priests and elders, who had turned against Jesus because of envy, were inciting the people to demand his death, and the people followed the edicts of the priests. Two, mob-behavior is seldom rational. Trigger one section with a slogan and the others follow. Their turn-coat behavior does not erase from memory, the adulation and accolades they gave Jesus when he walked with them. You will recall, that they wanted him to be their King.

"Jesus was a religious leader; we have no doubts. We have not gone into his religious teachings, except to center on his teaching that concerns us all. No man is an island. He needs people around him. It is, therefore, appropriate that he learns to live with them in a spirit of co-operation and co-existence, in a spirit of forgiveness, in perceiving the weaknesses of others with compassion, and in building bridges. Notice the way he reaches out to the thief on his right. Jesus has been tortured and tormented for several hours. He has not eaten. He has not slept. Every part of his body vibrates pain. Bleeding from wounds, his life is on the ebb. His friends have run away. The crowd mocks him: if you really are the miracle worker we have seen on our streets, come down from the cross. Pain and sorrow are his only companions. He feels abandoned by all. At this time, the thief on his right asks Jesus to remember him. Jesus forgets his own pain and looks at another in pain. He does not accuse the thief, instead, his heart goes out to him in friendship." Joseph trailed off.

He waited until he regained his voice, and asked in an emotion-charged voice, "Could there be a truer example of reaching out to others?" He paused again, "We have tried to look at how he did what he did? What was his style? What were his skills? How did his attitude affect his relationships? Were his habits different from those of other successful professionals? We have tried to appraise him, and a picture of Jesus is forming we cannot help but admire. A picture of a Master Model who forges and strengthens relationships. We have, no doubt, much to learn from him. His greatness and strength are like the ocean. We can dip our little buckets and draw out of it. Those buckets will suffice, as long as we do not stop drawing from the source."

"What was Jesus' formula to successful relationships? I asked myself that question many times and came up with a rather short answer: *The Golden Rule*. Do to others what you would want them to do to you. The Rule is born of intrinsic discipline. Quoting Scott Peck again, I shall reinforce the point, *'Without discipline, we can solve nothing'*. We want people to respect us, to listen to us, to give us affection, to trust us, and not to hurt us. If only we remember others want the same treatment from us, our double standards would vanish. Our relationships would thrive. We will excel in building good relationships because we exercise discipline. Jesus showed no foe could gain an advantage over him because of the discipline he had in blunting hate with love. In doing it, he was proactive, always taking the first step towards friendship. The disciples gained strength in the warmth of his personality. His customers found him disarmingly acceptable. That is why people said he did everything well, and they were spellbound."

"Put differently, we build strong relationships by living the Golden Rule, which is obeying Jesus' command to love others as we love ourselves. Undoubtedly, it is a tall order, an extremely difficult project to undertake. Yet, it makes sense to cherish the Golden Rule as a lofty goal and pursue it. Why? As humans, we believe we are masters of the world. As professionals, we imagine we can conquer the odds against us.

No wonder we try to attain the unattainable. We climb our mountains, we run our sprints in record-breaking time, we sail uncharted waters and we chase daunting targets. The quest for new frontiers never stops. Wasn't it Robert Browning who asked, *'Ah, but a man's reach should exceed his grasp, or what's a heaven for?'*

"The Golden Rule is like a mirror we hold up to expose what we try to disguise and conceal. There is much we do not want others to see. It is only when we are brutally honest, we come face-to-face with our real selves, warts and all. That is when we get our wings. Those wings will help us fly to places we have yet to visit. There is another reason why the Golden Rule is important. Dale Carnegie, in his very popular book, *"How to Win Friends and Influence People"*, states a few relevant facts. He writes, 2,500 years ago, Zoraster taught the Golden Rule to his followers in Persia. At about the same time, Buddha, in India, taught his disciples to value others as they value themselves. Confucius and Lao-Tzu, both in China, propagated the same idea. The Jews in their holy book support the same value. And, Hindus in their sacred scriptures uphold the same belief. Dale Carnegie is trying to tell us that Jesus was not alone in proposing the Golden Rule. Others shared the same belief. The Rule is universal. It cuts across cultures and travels across borders to appeal to all of humankind. And, we are part of humankind. Difficult though it seems, The Golden Rule should be our objective. Despite the injunction by other leaders, it is important to remember Jesus was the only one who stated the Rule in a positive manner. The others, like learners, proposed: 'Do not do evil --- . Avoiding the negative is easier than doing the positive."

"Of particular interest to us, at this stage, should be Jesus' injunction to pursue excellence and his Situational Management style. Remember how he exhorted his disciples: *'Be Perfect'*. His dictum to us is to strive for perfection. In our attempts, we may not succeed, but we ought to get up quickly and try again. Take us. Don't we let frustration get the better of us? How often we give up? How often we settle for second best? How often we take up a task ill-prepared? Certainly, we should seriously take, Jesus' call for perfection. Only then will our teammates and others, who transact with us, see in us something they admire and want to emulate."

"Situational Management stems from the vital fact that each of us is different, unique, and therefore to be dealt with carefully and differently. Whether we direct, coach, support or delegate, we need to understand the person we are transacting with, and adapt to the situation, using our best to bring out the best in him or her. When we follow that style, our customers, vendors, other agencies and our teammates will see a new way in the way we transact business, a personalized and purpose-driven style. Reflecting on Situational Management, we must ponder our understanding of delegation. We want our seniors to delegate to us unconditionally, which is not wrong. But what do we do when we have to delegate to those who report to us? Are we ready to let go? More often than not we make a mockery of the idea, only to be mocked at by those who suffer at our hands. Some alarm bells are ringing. Are we listening?"

Lambert answered the rhetorical question, "Mr. D'Cruz, be assured. We are listening to you and your message."

Joseph: "Thank you, Mr. Kurien. I am sure you are speaking for the team." He continued, "Let us get down to practical dimensions. Not all customers give us pleasure when we transact with them. Some, internal and external, are difficult, bent on making life hard for us. To transact with them we have two options, be equally difficult or be understanding. Being equally difficult is easy. Tit-for-tat is soaked in pleasure. We sense the thrill of exercising power over somebody. The very idea is pleasing. Yet, what is the result? Strained relationships and negative outcomes continue to challenge us. The irony in this option surfaces when that 'somebody' is more powerful. With those who are weak, we retaliate because we are not afraid of the consequences but, with powerful people, we tend to be cautious. For example, can I hit out at my boss? Can I offend a big and powerful customer who contributes hugely to my revenue? Can I abuse a Government Officer who refuses to see things the way I see them? No, those actions would not be prudent. So, I am forced to exercise restraint. I am compelled to look for other ways to handle the situation and reluctantly switch to the second option of being understanding. In other words, I force upon myself a course of action I had not chosen in the beginning. I wear a mask and pretend not to be myself. Jesus cautions us against such hypocrisy. He says the second option of trying to understand others is better and therefore to be chosen always, and not just because the first option is not suited to dealing with powerful people. Jesus urges us, whether they are weak or strong, try to understand your customers. Perhaps my customer has had a bad day, perhaps he has not fully understood the context, perhaps he is begging for some appreciation, perhaps, if I do not ridicule him, he will take off his mask, perhaps he is willing to transact with me, if only I unclench my fist."

"Let us not get Jesus wrong. He does not want us to assume a passive posture. No, on the contrary, he urges us to engage in debate, disagree when our beliefs are challenged, object to the distortion of facts and firmly counter injustice. Do all of this, he pleads, as long as we do not malign or denigrate those who disagree with us. It would not be right to impute bad faith, just because of disagreements. They should not lose their dignity because they choose to oppose us and hatred should not enter our hearts. What does understanding the customer mean? It is trying to step into his shoes, trying to look at things through his window. It is difficult because we are accustomed to looking at things through our windows. The irony is that we are ready to look through his window, only when circumstances force us into such a compromise."

"Jesus is trying to teach us to genuinely abandon retaliation and not to use it even as a strategy. Give others the benefit of the doubt. Try not to be rash in judging others. Be respectful, rather than impudent. Value relationships, he exhorts us. Whether I transact with my wife or child or peer or banker, Jesus entreats me to look into the eyes of the person before me. Don't I see my reflection in his or her eyes? He or she is another person like me with a set of problems, Jesus explains. If only I extend a hand in friendship, that very person could surprise me by taking it. Building happy relationships is not something that we do to others; it is something we do for ourselves. When we learn to govern our thoughts and behavior, we gain and others gain through our changed disposition. Great thinkers have told us, time and again, that when we are kind and helpful to others, we are being good to ourselves. From our own experiences, we know that it is true. Each time we performed a good deed, we were enriched."

"Our understanding of Relationship Management should be different from the common perception. Let me explain myself. Many companies direct their skill at relationship management to swing big deals with high-volume customers. Suave executives focus on those top customers who will generate big profits for them. These ambitious young people have little time or courtesy for small customers. The odd thing is their polished veneer peels off under stress. I shall not sit in judgment, as Jesus admonished. Each company should evolve strategies best suited to its needs. That is why I recommend we evolve a new strategy. Many companies focus on profits and strive to grab more profits. They have chosen the profit-focus-path. We have done the same, with mixed results. Now, it is time to change."

"I suggest we deliberately switch to the people-focus-path. When we focus on people, they will bring us profits. We too will reach the profit-destination, but by another route. No matter how good our products and how well-tested our systems, goods do not fly off shelves on their own. People must choose to sell. People must choose to buy. People matter.

Once they are satisfied, we will earn profits. The people-force will drive us to achieve results that exceed our expectations, because the means are as important as the end. When we look at the havoc caused in the Corporate World through compromises, we are baffled at the short-sighted behavior of the Captains of Industry. Their obsession with the profit made them myopic to the means of achieving it. The case of Goldman Sachs rocked the business world, as did the case of Satyam Computers, and Modi Diamonds, in India. The name of Ben Johnson, the athlete, comes to mind; more recently, the case of Lance Armstrong. The ball-tampering episode in Australian cricket is recent. They had a laudable goal of being the best, but they chose the wrong means and had to leave the scene in disgrace. Once again, we see that both the end and the means have to be right."

"In the final analysis, we must define our goals. Do we want to be ranked among the top ten, the top three, in the Pharmaceutical Industry? Do we want to give our shareholders the highest returns on their investment? Do we want to be a 'famous' company? I am not disparaging these objectives. I am only asking if they are worth pursuing, if compromises are to be made in our values. They are welcome as a bonus. I have not become a mystic. I try not to lose sight of our priorities. What are they?

First, to be regarded as a trusted Pharmaceutical company. The Medical Profession should know Mount Pharmaceuticals will not make a compromise on the health of patients; our products can be used without the slightest doubt.

Second, to give customers, who buy our products, the confidence that they are getting the best, the industry can provide.

Third, those who transact with the company can count on fair dealings and do repeat business with us in trust.

Fourth, those who join us as internal customers are proud to be associated with us and view their association with us as a long-term investment.

Fifth, we take on the role of leadership, not in chart-busting results, but in proving to Industry that value-driven performance is possible. Pursuing values is not a sign of weakness but strength.

I am aware these are long term goals. We will pursue them, even as we attempt short term objectives of successful new product launches, market penetration, and entering virgin markets. The main idea is to stay with the basics. What better basics can we follow than those Jesus gave us, those that have been tested over 2000 years?"

"You read of the conversation between the Editor in Chief of Harvard Business Review and the CEO of Merck Pharmaceuticals, in the material we gave you. Besides the striking points the CEO made, he defined the three essential tasks of a CEO:

1) Set a direction for the company.
2) Allocate resources to head in the direction to ensure high returns to society.
3) Employ the best people to achieve company objectives.

"In a small way, I've tried to follow his recommendations. Just a few moments ago. I pointed you in the direction we will take. Shortly, I shall spell out what the VPs and I plan to do to accelerate our growth. I delight in the fact that I have the right people in the right places. I am proud of you. The company is proud of you. Although there is a big gap between the size and stature of Merck and Mount Pharmaceuticals, I am happy we choose to follow a few common objectives."

"You have heard it said, it is not the heavy hunting that hurts the hoofs of the horse, it is the hammer, hammer on the hard highway. It applies to us also. The daily grind hurts us, not the new product launch, or the new market entry, or cross-selling to huge institutions. The big events keep us on our toes. Routine takes its toll. How often do we not take our relationships for granted when transacting with people? How often do we not believe that we know, and commit errors of judgment? How often do we not make mistakes and try to hide our lapses? How often do we not take half measures, when better steps are in order?" The list of such questions is endless. The point is the same, we make compromises. We do not give our best. Jesus makes his point clear, be perfect; try to do everything you do well. Jesus, the role model, the master manager, the tall professional and matchless communicator teaches both the novice and the veteran to get to the person behind the name, the individual behind the designation, the kernel inside the mass."

"Some will call us disruptors. The labels they fix on us, should not disturb our peace. Instead, we should draw comfort from the way we see ourselves. As long as we see ourselves as change-leaders, we shall be motivated to excel. Wasn't it Mahatma Gandhi who wrote: *'No one can harm you but yourself?'*

"The Partridge usually waddles around one square kilometer. But the Arctic Tern flies 70,000 kilometers in one year. Let our detractors take after the Partridge. We'd rather fly after the Arctic Tern, reminding ourselves we have to add muscle to our wings before we start the long flight."

Richard raised his hand: "May I make a point?"
"Certainly, right after we take a five-minute break," Joseph replied.

Chapter Eighteen: Having New Eyes

"The real voyage of discovery consists not in seeking new landscapes, but in having new eyes." Marcel Proust

After a short break, the group returned to the conference room. Richard made the point he wished to make before the break. "Talking of basics, I was pleasantly surprised to read the interesting and far-reaching comments made by Professor Ludo Van de Heyden. Deloitte, launching its Centre for Corporate Governance, put together a panel of experts to share thoughts on Corporate Governance after the financial crisis in the last decade. It was on this occasion that the Professor made some radical points: He said that the shareholders do not pay for everything; consumers do, the Public, from whom consumers are drawn, pays for everything. Logically, it is the Public interest, not that of the shareholders, that the Company should uphold. This is why he supports Public Capitalism in which the Company gives priority to profit for the whole society over profit for the shareholder. The Company's primary objective should be of long-term value creation and not shareholder value. This places on the Company the onus of clearly communicating its set of values to all concerned. He goes on to say the Company should attract only shareholders who share the same thinking and support the same professed values. If they don't agree, it is better for them to drop out. He doesn't stop there. He challenges the Company to get its employees to blow the whistle if the Company deviates from its avowed goals. To put a stamp of authority on his words, The Professor added he and his colleagues studied 15 German Manufacturers, whose results showed that the higher the Fair Process in Strategic Planning, the better the outcomes. The Professor was reinforcing the belief of Paul Polman, the past boss of Unilever when he declared he worked for the consumer and not the shareholder. We recall reading Polman's words in the reading material you gave us."

Joseph was impressed with Richard's timely reference. "Those brave words warm my heart, Mr. Rozario. I draw consolation from the fact we will not be called idiots because we are now in the company of wise men." Having commended Richard, Joseph added: "We should not delude ourselves. We are not going to change the way the world transacts. We can begin by changing ourselves, to become spheres of influence. A few who transact with us will be impacted by our changed behavior, and, in turn, become spheres of influence in their network of relationships. It is a long process. Links in a chain will be forged. Some of our external customers will want to do repeat business with us because they have had happy transactions with us. It will be the same with internal customers. The process will widen and cover more customers, inside and outside the company, if we are consistent."

"Jesus strikes us as a humble man. Even when he was rejected and assailed, he persevered in his attempts to reach out to people. We recall Judas, who was betraying Jesus, was in the Upper Room. Jesus astounds us with the example he set before the last supper; he washes the feet of his disciples, including those of Judas. I cannot think of any CEO who would do something similar. Jesus was from the royal household of King David, most of his disciples were fishermen. There was a huge class-divide. Yet, it did not stop him from performing the lowly act of washing their feet. He did it to tell his disciples that service was the expression of love, it bridges barriers."

"Man is enriched through humility, not impoverished. A little humility will do us no harm, especially when we try to reach out to others and are rebuffed. For example, we may try to befriend a colleague who spurns us. Building rapport with those who reject us is difficult. They need to be convinced that we are genuine, that we understand the way they feel and are ready to listen to their words and feelings. When we are rebuffed, take heart and try again. Our resolve to stay on course will be tested. Service, as a mark of our love and a reflection of our humility, is never easy."

"Allow me to digress for a moment. How many of you have watched the movie, Gone with the Wind?" A few hands went up. "A week ago, I viewed it for the second time. It is an old movie on old times, a story of romance against the backdrop of the American Civil War. Without my knowing it, I was drawn to the old-world charm. To those who have not seen it, I strongly recommend the movie.

Of the many things that struck me, the contrast between the two women characters was significant. There is Scarlett, spitting fire, manipulating people and managing situations to her advantage. In beautiful contrast is Melanie, her sister-in-law. She can think no evil, speak no unkind word and do no uncharitable act, even against Scarlett who feigns affection. Her life is a litany of kind words and generous deeds. Her humility is praiseworthy. Whom shall we follow? Scarlett, who scattered scorn and gathered ill will or Melanie, who sowed kindness and reaped goodwill? The answer is obvious.

Jesus spoke of choosing the narrow path, the difficult path, over the broad road. Scarlett chose the broad road to self-satisfaction, getting what she wanted. But was she happy? One wonders. Melanie chose the narrow path, finding happiness in the happiness of others, the difficult path. One could pooh-pooh this as an example drawn from the celluloid world. Fine."

"Let us take a real-life example. Mother Teresa was celebrated for the good work she did across the world but, to those who knew her better, what she gave each person mattered most to her. When she was interacting with a person, she gave that person her everything. The need of the person got her full attention. At that time, nothing else was important. As a result, each transaction was enriching. People were enthralled, just to have a word with her. She summed up her belief when she said, *'Love is giving the best we have.'* The late J. R. D. Tata, the uncle of Ratan Tata, was known to have the same attitude. Whether he was speaking with his chauffeur or one of the top executives, in his Industrial Empire, he gave his all to the person in front of him. We know how successful he was. What am I trying to convey to you?"

"Even in the hard-nosed commercial world, there is room for understanding. There is scope for the win-win attitude. If we choose to bring to the table our all, holding nothing back, there is a fair chance the outcome of the transaction will be better than expected. Customer or friend, the act of dealing with him in humility and sincerity makes a difference. That is something Jesus teaches us."

"In the extra reading material, which you received and read, there was a set of papers on the humanity of Jesus. You read of his superior intelligence, emotional intelligence, and spiritual intelligence. What do we infer? When we improve our emotional and spiritual intelligence (scored as EQ and SQ), through focused effort, we too can build better relationships. Now, it is for us to tear down the walls separating us and build bridges with those around us, starting with those in this conference room."

"You can say that again," echoed Anjali.

Joseph smiled broadly and continued, "Ladies and gentlemen, I have been speaking to you from my head and my heart. Although I did prepare for this session, I must confess, at times my heart took over. Why did that happen? The answer is Jesus' teaching touched my heart. I hope it touches yours, too. Once you let him touch your heart, his words will find a way to your head. They are in my head now. Let me clarify what I just said. From my business school days, I may have read in excess of one thousand books on Management and Self-Development. I am not referring to books on Science and Systems, but to those on thought-patterns. I have attended scores of seminars and read many hundred articles on such subjects. Never once have I been influenced as I was when I read The Gospels. I'll tell you why. Jesus is strikingly original, both in his words and deeds. He has not copied anyone. Instead, he gave the Golden Rule body and soul. I am open to correction on what I am about to state.

The books I have read, even by celebrated authors, are not original. Directly or indirectly, knowingly or unknowingly, they have borrowed thoughts from The Gospels. They have recycled, refashioned, extended or elaborated on those thoughts and given them labels, nice-sounding names. It is not that they plagiarized or engaged in something unlawful. No, it is just that they plucked at an idea already in circulation, an idea 2000 years old. In sharp contrast, Jesus stands alone in majestic splendor, not influenced by those who went before him or his contemporaries."

"It is true, some thinkers, who lived before Jesus gave us some lofty thoughts and important messages. But most of them speak or write like learners who painstakingly arrive at some conclusions, which they share with us. Many of those thoughts are enlightening but don't tell the whole story. Rays from the rising sun give light, but dark shadows fall in many places. Jesus is different, he is like the sun at noon, brightening half the world at the same time. He speaks with authority, and his words have finality. He is not the hard-working learner, whom we recognize in some thinkers, but the peerless teacher, who stands apart. He understands the human predicament, the hard choices we have to make and our struggle. That is why he answers tricky questions and gives us complete messages. In short, he offers a breathtakingly refreshing new way of life. Really, he has no peers, because by example he showed how his lessons could be followed.

True wisdom offers not just great thoughts, but great deeds as well. He lived what he taught. From what I have seen, history has not thrown up another who has been so faithful and so consistent. No wonder his words have found a way to my head. I will join the Temple Police in saying no one has spoken like him, and the crowds that said *he did all things well*."

"What are Nelson Mandela's words? *'A good head and a good heart are always a powerful combination.'* He should know. Let the head and heart combination work for us. Let us dare to be different in adopting people-focused policies and practices, starting with the 360-degree Appraisal. Let it not be said of us that we feared and therefore did not attempt."

"Someone said a newspaper is the first draft of history. What we do now will be the first draft of the history of Mount Pharmaceuticals. History does not lie. It does not take sides. Ten years down the line, what will the history of our company tell those who come after us? Like our predecessors, we chose to walk the safe and beaten track, or will it record our attempts to walk the narrow-less-traveled path? Will our names be written in gold?"

He stopped, sipped some water and looked up. "I must share something more with you. Right through our discussions, the VP's and I have had to resolve differences. Some of us believed we had no business to drag Jesus into Corporate affairs. Some thought the idea was too radical to be practical. Jesus, a religious head, was too ancient to be a model for us today. Is he relevant? Some of you also voiced similar reservations. I am glad you did since I would not want you to accept the idea just because I proposed it. I would want you to think about it. Debate it. Happily, it turned outright, not because of our persuasive skills, far from it. At best we could take credit for begging you to read the New Testament and the other articles. All the persuasion you needed came from the Gospels, from the person of Jesus, and from what others had to say of Jesus. It seemed so easy once you read the Gospels. Just as effectively as he handled objections from people of his time, he would have answered questions that occurred to you as you read the Gospels. He astounded them; he had you amazed.
People like Mahatma Gandhi, Swami Vivekananda and stalwarts like them were edified when they met Jesus in the Gospels. So, you are in good company."

Joseph stopped and said, "If you have any questions, I shall be happy to answer them."
Sammy spoke for the first time: "What happens next?"
Joseph responded: "Mr. Rozario is trying to put some order into our various discussions. He is also doing some independent investigation. A few weeks from now, when he is ready, we shall announce the start of the 180-degree appraisal. In phases, we shall go to 270-degree and 360-degree. It is one plan of action."
"The other is to introspect. We recall the parable Jesus told of the farmer scattering seeds. Seeds falling on hard ground did not take root, while seeds that fell on fertile soil took root and yielded a rich harvest. The parable applies to us. When our minds are prepared, we will benefit from the wisdom in the Gospels. If we refuse to condition our minds, only we will be the losers. Try to understand me. I am not suggesting anything new or radical. These ideas are 2000 years old. Sadly, we did not recognize them earlier. Peter Drucker was right when he wrote,

decades ago, that doing the right thing is more important than doing things right. This nugget of wisdom cannot be ignored. He too, like others in his league, was rephrasing the wisdom of Jesus. It is time we did the right things."

"As some of you know, I have read the Gospels four times. I am looking forward to reading it for the fifth time. May I suggest we read and re-read the Gospels and the material we have with us? I mean ponder the Gospels, as we would a book of special interest to us, and not as a religious text, and discover the wisdom in them. Then let us examine our own strengths and weaknesses, against a checklist of points we have from the appraisal of Jesus. Let us check our own relationship-building efforts. How do we compare? There is one question we could repeatedly ask ourselves in different situations: **What would Jesus have done in such a situation?** An answer can help us work on some of our deficiencies so that, in time, we become professionals who better handle our relationships. In time, our seniors, peers, juniors, and customers will give us a better appraisal."

"To improve the relationship with our peers, we will follow the suggestion made by Katie Burke, Chief People Officer, Hubspot. She makes a strong case for rotating the seating arrangement in the office. When we rotate the seating arrangement, we get a new set of neighbors in the office. Then we have a chance to cultivate new relationships, instead of staying with the same set of old neighbors. To lend a new dimension to her proposal, those of us who occupy cabins will move into the open office. When we need to discuss important points, we can move into the conference room for the discussion. Let us tear down the walls that separate us."

"Yet another plan is to relook at everything that happens in the company. After the launch of the 180-degree Appraisal, which will happen in a few weeks, the VP's and I will rewrite our policies to make them more customer-friendly – internal and external. One step in the direction will be the rationalizing and restructuring of the compensation-packages for the internal customers. Jesus said the laborer should receive food and a just wage. This will happen in April next year. We have already started work on this big project. Even as it gets underway, we will scrutinize every single operation in the company to rid ourselves of customer-unfriendly practices, make our manufacturing processes more environment-friendly, bring in more transparency, and try to lift our dealings to a level above reproach. We will take action on a war-footing, to solve even problems from minor customer-dissatisfaction. Training and retraining will get an impetus structured to suit specific needs. The changes we make will benefit both internal and external customers. The major revamping exercise will take some time, but our efforts will be unrelenting."

"I will place all our plans, old wine in new skins, to borrow a phrase from Jesus, before the Board of Directors. With the support of some like-minded gentlemen on the Board, I expect to win the Board's approval. Mr. Marcus Gomes, a large shareholder, is already working on our behalf with other Board Members. We all know Mr. Marcus Gomes is powerful."

"I can feel the winds of change blowing in my face and I like the feel. But change is not going to be easy. We will face stiff opposition inside and outside the company. Our plans will be scoffed at, our actions derided and the results we produce belittled. Changing others to our way of thinking is going to take time. Until then it will be a lonely walk down a narrow path, where our character will be on display. I hope we will not be found wanting. To combat the assault on the choices we make, we shall launch an assertive Public Relations Campaign, which hopefully will counter the propaganda against us. Besides, the PR Program will pump some buoyancy into the Stock Market."

"Speaking of buoyancy, I am thrilled at the idea that our leadership could lend some cheer to those who wish to learn. I had in mind other corporations and professionals, in general. I have not known of any team in the Industrial World consciously choosing to follow Jesus' Golden Rule. I have known of Christian Congregations and Groups who have tried. Some of them succeeded in part, many did not because of the compulsions and temptations in daily life. People outside the religious fold have not made it their driving principle. Imagine what change can come about when doctors, attorneys, judges, consultants, professors, media managers, bankers, retailers, salespersons, and service providers join our ranks! How different transactions will be!

"When the mindset is changed, the conversion will be easier. People need to be convinced that The Golden Rule is in their interest. Long-term gains and enduring relationships can be built only through understanding, politeness and the following of Jesus' basic teachings. Your customer, internal or external, will be good if you are good to him. You cannot dispute that. Unless you are fair and polite in your dealings you cannot expect your customer to transact with you again. Can you disagree? Once professionals like us stop to think, the logic in Jesus' words cannot be refuted. The problem is in stopping to think when we are in a mad rush to make more and more money. I am hopeful the change will come, though slowly, when we all try. I shall be using every forum I have to speak and write, to put across my conviction. Forgive me, our conviction. I urge each of you to seize every opportunity you get to spread the word."

"We owe it to ourselves and to Jesus. In a way, informing and persuading others in our fraternity could be part of our mission. The task is huge, but the rewards are great. While we are busy propagating the new role of the professional, we should redefine professionalism. Qualifications, experience, skills, commitment, and competence are important; but not enough. In your discussions yesterday, you agreed that a professional should optimize the use of resources. The question is: How does he do it? So, the means he adopts, to optimize the use of his resources, become vital. Therefore, the picture of the professional is incomplete without the finishing stroke of the brush. Unless he can put life into his relationships, by forging lasting and fulfilling relationships, his profile is incomplete and imperfect. To us, professionalism will be the achieving of our goals through empowered professional relationships, living the Golden Rule. At Mount Pharmaceuticals we shall try to perfect our profiles. And, with constant effort, we shall try to influence others."

Looking at his notes, Joseph continued: "Some of you in the Marketing Team may harbor reservations. We will try to understand any dissenting voice, as long as the voice is clear and truthful. Please feel free to speak with your boss. You know my door is also open to you. Let me correct myself: You are welcome to my table in the open office. We shall listen to your problems. We shall try to marshal facts to convince you. If your fears are deep-seated, we may not succeed in our attempts. On this account, be assured neither your day-to-day functioning nor your career advancement will be at stake. We are with you as you are with us, even if we choose to disagree on some points. We respect you as you respect us.

May I draw your attention to the article *"Respect in the Corporation"* by Kristie Rogers? It appeared in the Harvard Business Review of July-August 2018. Reference to the article is in the material we gave you. However, once a policy decision is taken, as a professional, please do your duty. At this point, we need to remind ourselves of the controversial statement made by Eldridge Cleaver: *'If you are not part of the solution, then you are part of the problem'*. None of us wants to be part of the problem, rather, we shall be part of the solution of making Mount Pharmaceuticals a unique corporation, powered by Jesus' Golden Rule. For my part, I shall lead you in this path-breaking endeavor. It is a promise." Pausing, Joseph concluded: "Mr. Samir Ghosh, since I have answered your question, I take it that we can close the session. I would not want to keep you for more than three hours. It was my promise to you yesterday."

There was prolonged applause when Joseph ended his impassioned presentation. He went around shaking hands and thanking each participant for the support he received. Then, he led the Vice Presidents out of the room. The Marketing Managers and the Regional Managers were to meet for dinner at Lambert's home later in the evening. In a more relaxed atmosphere, they would air some of their private views. Lambert would be ready for them.

"May I walk you down to your car?" Joseph asked Lambert.
"Thank you, you look tired. Why don't you go home and get some sleep?" Lambert pleaded.
"No problem. Give me the pleasure," Joseph appealed.
"What pleases you, pleases me," Lambert teased; and changing tone, continued: "You were fantastic! Absolutely fantastic! You had us enthralled, begging for more. You know something, if Christians reflected on the Gospels the way you have, the world would be a changed place. The next time I read the Gospels, it will be through your reading glasses."
"Thank you, Lambert. These thoughts have taken root in me. I am trying to let them grow and blossom. You were lucid in your presentation. Connecting Jesus with marketing was a masterstroke. Now that the conference is over, let us get to other things. When are you getting Augustus his bicycle?"
"Thank you for commending my presentation. It is kind of you. In a day or two I will get Augustus his bicycle," Lambert said.
"What Christmas gift has Lissy planned for you?" Joseph probed.
"She says it will be a surprise," Lambert seemed pleased with the prospect.
"Allow me also to surprise you with a Christmas gift," Joseph petitioned.
"What did you have in mind?" Lambert was curious.
"Nothing very glamorous or high priced," Joseph said modestly.
"I can't wait longer, tell me," Lambert entreated.
"On Monday, two weeks from the time we first met to discuss your appraisal, we shall finish it," Joseph said.
"Thank you," Lambert sighed.
Joseph, looking into the near future, declared, "Lambert, next year you will benefit from the 180-degree Appraisal. Your peers will definitely give you bonus points."
"I will be happy to take them on board," Lambert replied, smiling broadly.

References: Books

* The Holy Bible, The New Revised Standard Version, Catholic Edition for India Published by Thomas Nelson for Theological, Publications in India, Bangalore (India)." The Scripture quotations contained herein are from the New Revised Standard Version Bible: Catholic Edition. Copyright (c) 1993 and 1989 by the Division of Christian Education of National Council of the Churches of Christ in the USA. Used by permission. All rights reserved".
* The Family Devotional Bible Study, India Bible Literature, Post Bag 459, Madras (India).
* A case for Christ, by Lee Strobel, Published by Zondervan.
* Life of Christ by Fulton J. Sheen, Asian Trading Corporation, Bangalore (India)
* Jesus the Teacher, by Brian Grenier, St. Paul Publications, Bombay (India).
* What think you of Christ? by Ian Travers-Ball, S.J., St. Paul Publication, Bombay (India).
* Responses to 101 questions about Jesus, by Michael L. Cook, S.J St. Paul Publication, Bombay
* The Nazarene (Vol. I) by S.D. Arul Nathan, 4/39-1, St. Patrick Church Road, St. Thomas Mount, Madras (India).
* The Tour of the Summa of Saint Thomas Aquinas, by Paul J. Glenn, Theological Publications in India, Bangalore (India)
* Essentials of Management, by Harold Koontz and Heinz Weihrich, McGraw Hill International Edn.
* Leadership and the one Minute Manager, by Kenneth Blanchard, Patricia Zigarmi, Drea Zigarmi. Witham Morrow & Co. Inc. New York.
* The Peter Principle, by Dr. Lawrence J. Peter, Bantam Books
* Up the Organization, by Robert Townsend, Coronet Books, Hodder Fawcett Ltd., London
* How to conduct Staff Appraisals, by Nigel Hunt, How to Books Ltd., Plymouth, United Kingdom
* Turned On, by Roger Dow and Susan Cook, Harper Business
* You Can Win - A step by step tool for top achievers, by Shiva Khera, Macmillan India Ltd.,

References: Articles

- How to run a business inspired by faith, Robert L Kinast and Judith Schloegel – (The New Leader Magazine)
- The 360 degree Technique - Anshun Tandon - (Business Today)
- All those in favor, say Aye R. Mahalaxmi - (Economic Times)
- The New People Economy, Sundeep Khanna- (Business Today)
- The right shift - Attitude is the key determinant of a successful business leader
  A. Thothathri Raman- (Business India)
- How good is your EQ? Radha Dhawan - (Business World)
- Emotions score over Intelligence, Ashoke K. Maitra - (Economic Times)
- Harvard Business Review – March-April 2018

Author Page

Greetings!

I thank you for the interest you have shown in my book. If you liked what you read in JESUS CHRIST IN THE BUSINESS WORLD, please tell others. Please share your thoughts by way of a short review on Amazon.

My website www.ignatiusfernandez.com hosts the link to the Amazon Page.

Thank you for your time and indulgence. God bless you and yours.

~Ignatius Fernandez

He was in Industry for thirty years. Rising from the ranks, he operated as General Manager, Director, and Chief Executive. Later, he moved to academics to be a Professor of Management in Business Schools and Corporate Trainer for senior managers. As a speaker, counselor for families, blogger, and author, he added facets to his profile.

Other books by the author:
- Meeting Jesus in the Holy Land
- Think CHRIST, Live Christian
- Jesus Christ – True Leader and Perfect Gentleman
- The Child is Father of the Man – Tips and Techniques for Wise Parenting
- The Golden Rule – For Empowering Professional Relationships
- The Heart has its Reasons – Looking Back Looking Ahead
- Life Lessons – A Christian Sharing
- Through the Eye of a Needle – Transforming Relationships
- Relationship Management – The Master's Way
- My Family – The Next Best Thing That Happened to Me

And, over sixty of his articles appear in magazines and on international websites.

Facebook:
https://www.facebook.com/ignatius.fernandez.3

LinkedIn:
https://www.linkedin.com/in/ignatius-fernandez

Lightning Source UK Ltd.
Milton Keynes UK
UKHW050628240220
359147UK00009B/66